SICK HOUSES

SICK HOUSES

Haunted Homes & The Architecture Of Dread

Leila Taylor

Published by Repeater Books

An imprint of Watkins Media Ltd

Unit 11 Shepperton House

89-93 Shepperton Road

London

N1 3DF

United Kingdom

www.repeaterbooks.com

A Repeater Books paperback original 2025

1

Distributed in the United States by Random House, Inc., New York.

ISBN: 9781915672636

Ebook ISBN: 9781915672643

Printed and bound by CPI Group (UK) Ltd, Croydon, CR0 4YY

Table of Contents

"A deranged house is a pretty conceit."
The Haunting of Hill House, Shirley Jackson

Introduction:
The Unhappy House

Shirley Jackson kept postcards and photos of old houses pinned on the wall above her typewriter, a collection of images for her stories that often revolved around houses. I also collect houses. There are some that give me a spark, a bit of a twinge, a racing heart for no reason. There's the house a few blocks away that looks abandoned but isn't; there's the top floor of a mansard roof in the Flatiron District painted solid matte black; a farmhouse I once passed staring out of the window in the back seat on a road trip, peeling grey and nearly falling over. I'm drawn to houses that feel wrong for whatever reason.

I found this house by chance doing an image search for something else. It's an old house on a street in New Orleans and I've named it the Pink Half-House. It freaked me out the moment I saw it, but I couldn't pinpoint exactly why. I'll describe it this way: Start with the silhouette of a house. You know the one: a square with a triangle on top. Now, starting at the top, slice it in half, from the point of the roof down to the street. You can throw the left half away. It's painted a salmon pink color that has peeled off in large chunks. There is a grey metal garage door that takes up almost the entire width of the building, newer looking but worn out and a little banged up. Above it is a window that looks original to me; I'm guessing mid-1800s: tall, nearly the height of the story, narrow, with closed shutters painted grey. Extended out to the right of the house is a high wall, nine, maybe ten feet tall, painted the same pink color and connected to another, larger house with a normal façade. It was a strange configuration that just looked wrong, and I got a little obsessed with it. I found out why it gave me the creeps. What I was looking at was an urban slave quarter.

New Orleans Slave House, Grant Groberg, 2006

What we would consider the front of the house was turned inward toward the courtyard facing the big house. The wall enclosed the two houses in one compound. The pitch of the roof was highest at its outer edge, sloping down like a bended head to the house across. The Pink Half-House had no front door because it was not an autonomous house but an appendage of the other. It didn't face the street, but the house it served. The two were not equal in height: the ceilings of the slave quarters were lower, so if you were standing on the second-floor balcony you would have to look up at the second floor of the big house. It's a diabolical design, the form of the house itself subservient. A sick house.

Out of all the genres and variations of horror, the haunted house is my favorite. Since the first gothic novel, *The Castle of Otranto* by Horace Walpole, the provenance of horror has been the home. It's an obvious starting point, because the home is the provenance of ourselves. Our home is, or should be, our sanctuary, our designated center of comfort, security, and respite, a place where we are naked, literally and emotionally. You are safe at homebase.

The haunted house endures because out of all the arenas where horror may play out, the home is the one closest to us. The house is, as Gaston Bachelard puts it, "the topography of our intimate being," an externalization of ourselves containing the materiality of our identity. It is the place where we mark our history and frame our future. Our homes *are* us, and we talk about people we love as being home to us. Home is where the heart is and there's no place like it. I'm also a big fan of possession and exorcism movies for this same reason. When a demon inhabits a body, it takes ownership of a person; a monster is temporarily housed inside of its victim, our body invaded, repossessed. The ghost does the same with a house: it breaks into it, takes possession of what is yours, and you can no longer trust the place you trusted the most. What's more frightening than your own home turning against you?

Not all the houses in my collection are haunted, or if they are I'm not aware of it. Some are fictional, horror movie, and fairytale houses. Some are real houses that became infamous because of the people who resided within them. Imagined houses are often borrowed from real places, fictional characters resembling actual buildings, living or dead. There are dollhouses, miniature surrogates for the home. There are apartment buildings housing thousands, and cabins meant only for one. The commonality among them is an uncanny quality of unease in a space designed for comfort, the *unheimlich* un-homeyness of the alienated house. They are houses that, for one reason or another, for better or worse, are "bad" in some way. They're houses that haunt me.

This book is a catalog of houses that have gone wrong and the ways our built environment can evoke terror and dread. But more so this is a book about the home, and the idea of home, and how horror perverts and manipulates one of the most personal and intimate experiences we have as human beings. "Home" is a feeling, not an object. It's for that reason I don't talk about some of the more usual suspects. I'm not talking about plantation houses because: 1.) fuck them, and 2.) I don't consider slave quarters homes. I don't talk about prisons or hotels (I'll save H.H. Holmes for another day). A residence isn't necessarily a home. It's not enough for a structure to look creepy, oppressive, or foreboding. It must belong to someone. Someone has to claim it as their own and expect to find comfort and security there. In *The Haunting of Hill House*, Eleanor Vance says, "I'm expected," six times before she even walks through the doors. Isn't that what a home is? A place where one is expected?

.

American Houses

The Great Suggestion

"A nation of homeowners, of people who own a real share in their own land, is unconquerable."

> — President Franklin D. Roosevelt, message to the United States Savings and Loan League (1942)

"I think I want my family and my children much more than a structure."

> — Kathy Lutz, *Amityville: An Origin Story* (2023)

Before all hell quite literally busts loose in Stuart Rosenberg's *The Amityville Horror* (1979), George Lutz (James Brolin) scoffs at his wife Kathy's (Margot Kidder) desire to have their new home blessed. "This is a big event in my family," she says. "We've always been a bunch of renters. This is the first time anyone's bought a house." She says "a bunch of renters" with a piteous tone I find a bit offensive. I've never owned a house and never personally felt the need to, but I see the appeal. It would be nice to have a place where I can change the kitchen cabinets, re-tile the bathroom floor and paint the walls black (or a very deep, velvety blue — I have thought about this) without having to worry about returning it to white. To have a place I can make indelible marks upon without ramification and to have the stability of a mortgage instead of the uncertain temporality of a lease. There is a permanence to ownership that I have yet to appreciate, and a level of commitment to place that I have yet to reach. I'm always impressed when a friend buys their home, but it's never been a goal of mine. That being said, I've also never been very good at financial planning. But I get where Kathy is coming from; it *is* a big deal. For the Lutzes, it's a sign that they've *made* it, they've crossed another milestone on the path toward social establishment and upward mobility. She's a grown-ass woman with three kids, a burly husband, and a five-bedroom Dutch Colonial in the suburbs. She is one step closer to what Lauren Berlant calls "that moral-intimate-economic thing called 'the good life.'"[1]

For most people, buying a home is a big event, perhaps one of the biggest, and that promise of financial stability and progress is one Americans have been taught to desire. Homeownership signifies a stable income, a cohesive family unit, a valued place in society, personal security, and, most importantly, agency. Homeownership provides the comfort that there is one place, at the very least, where we are in control, whatever the square footage. Loss of agency is at the heart of every haunted house story (and horror in general). The haunting shatters the illusion that we have control over our spaces; suddenly that which we consider ours is inexplicably not. In a haunting, what we do, where we go, and how we live become dictated by a force beyond our comprehension, a phantasmagoric home invasion that is impossible to predict or defend against. There's no home security system that protects against ghosts. The walls we paint, the rooms we nest in, the space in which we plant our personal flags aren't ours alone, and something alien is messing with our stuff. In a haunting, we lose dominion over our personal chunk of the world, and we are suddenly much smaller and weaker than we ever thought we were. But before the walls start bleeding, while the kids romp in the lake with the dog and Kathy struggles with the shelf paper, we're happy for them and their American Dream come true, and we fear for them since we know what they have to lose.

There has been an aspirational, glorified rhetoric around the idea of the home for a while — since the Victorian age and the relatively new importance put on the nuclear family. Home became "the quiet repository of man's fondest hopes and the cherished sanctuary of Earthly happiness." [2] The home became sanctified, something to be protected and preserved at all costs. It was the material bedrock of one's very existence and became synonymous with family.

Haunted house movies work because they usually start with a family and a baseline of identifiable normalcy. Its why Tobe Hooper's *Poltergeist* (1982) is so effective. The Freelings are extremely ordinary, not perfect; just an ordinary American family. Diane (JoBeth Williams) is a laid-back stay-at-home mom; Steve (Craig T. Nelson) is a father with a good job who loves his family; they have good kids with just the right amount of sass, and, of course, a golden retriever. The house is a bit messy, with the normal amount of chaos for a family of five. There's no significant familial strife and whatever problems they have are ordinary. In bed, mom rolls a joint while dad reads Ronald Reagan's biography. Everything is unmistakably unexceptional until the "tv people" instantaneously rearrange their kitchen chairs into a physics-defying sculpture and an invisible force drags their five-year-old daughter, Carol Ann (Heather O'Rourke), from one end of the kitchen floor to the other. The terrors that the Freeling family endure over the next hour and a half are all the more frightening because there is nothing extraordinary about their family. They are relatable. It could happen to anyone.

In the horror genre, the "typical American family" has been overwhelmingly white, straight, cis-gendered and middle to lower-middle class, composed of a mother, father, and a few kids (and maybe a golden retriever). One of the reasons Jordan Peele's *Us* (2019) stands out in the genre is that it centers an ordinary, middle-class, nuclear family — mother, father, and two kids — who happen to be Black. The Wilsons, Gabe (Winston Duke) and Adelaide (Lupita Nyong'o), have a loving marriage. Dad is a proud Howard University alum; mom is affectionate if a bit over-protective. The kids, Zora (Shahadi Wright Joseph) and Jason (Evan Alex), are smart, with their own quirky idiosyncrasies. They make enough money for a summer home but not enough to buy a decent boat. But while they've been living out the middle-class American dream, below ground their doppelgangers have been living a nightmare, waiting to take it back, for their time in the sun.

The conceit of homeownership and personal prosperity, of the "American Dream," is a relatively new one. It's always signified success, and what success looks like has changed throughout the years. But it has always been a myth. The original dream was not about personal prosperity but democratic equality: life, liberty, the pursuit of happiness, and all that. From the start it was a flawed idea, since the "we" in "we the people" only meant white men; specifically white men who owned property. It was always about property, no matter how lofty the language. There is also the Emma Lazarus dream of America as a land of plenty, beaconing "the huddled masses yearning to breathe free," but we've always been rather picky about which of the "homeless, tempest-tossed" we welcome, and for those who moved through Ellis

Island and into the tenements of the Lower East Side, the vision of a land of opportunity faded fast.

American Homes and Gardens, 1905; *House & Garden*, 1921; and *The House Beautiful*, 1912

Then, at the beginning of the twentieth century, people got a look at how the other half lived. On the movie screen and in newspaper advertisements and the full-color photos of *Better Homes and Gardens* (better than yours, anyway), "ordinary Americans could scrutinize the lives of the rich and powerful in all their glamorous and luxurious detail."[3] After WWII and the economic boom that followed it, "the American Dream" became a slogan for individual prosperity and a capitalist rallying cry against the Red Scare. Since then, the phrase has come to define a nationalistic ideology founded on personal wealth so ingrained in our culture that it's come to define what it means to be a citizen.

A dream can be a guiding aspiration, or it can be a puerile illusion; sometimes it can be both at the same time. The American Dream is the promise that, regardless of your social, ethnic, religious, or economic origins, financial prosperity and the power that comes with it can be yours. Social scientist Jennifer Hochschild calls it "the great national suggestion," [4] that if you work hard and play by the rules, upward mobility in the form of a detached single-family house can be yours. Maybe. It depends.

In the 1930s, during the Great Depression, President Franklin D. Roosevelt established the Federal Housing Administration and signed the Housing Act as part of the New Deal. In an effort to boost residential construction and homeownership, the federally secured mortgage was established to allow people with smaller incomes to get loans to buy homes. When the GI Bill was introduced after WWII, a returning vet could buy a house for just $100 down and $100 a month. Owning a house became a real, attainable goal for more people than ever before (or rather, for some people), and the white, middle-class, suburban nuclear family with a house and a mortgage became the blueprint for the United States citizen.

Levittown houses/ Gottscho-Schleisner Collection
(Library of Congress)

Abraham Levitt — the creator of the planned community of

mass-produced houses known as Levittown — said, "No man who owns a home can be a communist, because he has too much to do."[5] I'm not sure why Levitt assumed communists aren't busy, but they weren't the only ones not welcome in Levittown: Black folks were banned outright. The GI Bill didn't explicitly exclude Black veterans, but Jim Crow laws, redlining, and discriminatory lending practices did just that. The Federal Housing Administration established a new criteria for approving mortgages with credit and collateral standards that eliminated many Black households from qualification. Predominantly Black neighborhoods were classified by the banks as high-risk, even dangerous, resulting in blatant racial segregation and a concentration of poverty.

From the start, agency, representation, legacy, and even humanity were tied to the ability to own one's land. In 1856, Walt Whitman wrote an essay decrying the condition of tenement living in New York City:

> *A man is not a whole and complete man unless he owns a house and the ground it stands on. Men are created owners of the earth. Each was intended to possess his piece of it; and however the modifications of civilized life have covered this truth, or changed the present phase of it, it is still indicated by the universal instinctive desire for landed property, and by the fuller sense of independent manhood which comes from the possession of it.*[6]

Whitman suggests an almost divine right to property as a sign of full personhood. He wrote that essay about a decade before the Thirteenth Amendment was signed, in 1865, abolishing slavery. The Southern Homestead Act would be signed a year later, granting Black people full citizenship and the right to buy property of their own. If you were a single woman, you'd have to wait until 1974 before you could get a loan to buy a house; before then, you'd need your husband's signature. Not everyone had access to this "dream," and some actively resisted it. The idealized image of patriarchal domesticity was something early feminists vehemently fought against. Centering the house as the primary space, or the only space for women, meant that for some, the home was not a sanctuary to retreat to but something to escape from. Before ghosts and poltergeists even enter the picture, the foundation of homeownership as an ideal condition was always shaky at best.

There is an identity attached to homeownership, a co-habitation of the self and the architecture. You are a homeowner, not a houseowner. We don't go to haunted homes on Halloween, and it's not the *Haunting of Hill Home*. A house is a thing made of wood, brick, drywall, and glass. A home is a state of being. A house doesn't become a home until it's claimed, occupied, until the territory has been marked, until you feel comfortable, safe, until you *feel at* home.

The first night in a new place is always a bit weird. After a long day of moving boxes from one place to another, you get take-out for dinner at an unfamiliar restaurant, and you unpack the bare necessities and begin placing things in temporary new spots until you find a place for them. With the table lamps still packed, you turn off the harsh overhead light and get into your familiar bed in its unfamiliar space and see the room in darkness for the first time. The windows without curtains cast strange shadows; you hear little noises you never heard before in daylight. Are they coming from inside or outside? It's yours technically: you signed the paperwork, made the deposit, you have the keys. But it's not home. Not yet. I imagine that discomfort, that feeling of displacement in your own space, is what a haunting must feel like, to be exposed without the protection of familiarity. In a haunting, a process of depersonalization takes place. A monsterization. It's not only about what makes a house a home but what turns a home back into a house.

House, Sweet House

"I want to be a white dad in a horror movie, currently moving my brunette wife and our dejected children into an abandoned ghost factory for a fresh start."

— weaver-z, tumblr.com, 14 September 2021

There is a typical formula to the start of haunted house movies, starting with the journey to the new house. Usually, it's in a car. Here we're introduced to the family, usually Dad at the wheel, Mom riding shotgun, and a couple of kids in the backseat, often a surly teenager with headphones and a sweet and eager little brother or sister. A sweeping overhead drone (or helicopter back in the day) hovers above a sedan, following it along a winding road surrounded by trees. A lone yellow VW bug zooms along Sidewinder Road on its way to the Overlook Hotel in *The Shining*. The couple sing along to the Specials on the radio in *Vivarium* or to Luniz in *Us*. The city kids marvel at all the trees and the teenager sulks over leaving all their friends behind. Even Robert Eggers gives us the seventeenth-century version in a horse-drawn cart in *The Witch*, complete with a surly teenager in the back. I have my own memories, from the back seat of our Honda Accord, of the journey from my family's home in Massachusetts to our new house in Michigan, the trunk filled to capacity, a cargo carrier strapped to the roof, and the occasional pit-stop at Howard Johnson's.

The family is leaving something behind and looking forward to a fresh start. They are in that liminal space between the familiar and the new. It's all potential at this point. In *American Horror Story: Murder House*, the Harmon family is moving after the mother has had a miscarriage and the father had an affair. In *The Messengers*, a family is moving to start a sunflower farm to help pay for their son's medical expenses. In *The Remains*, the dad is recently widowed. In the 2015 remake of *Poltergeist*, the father was recently laid off, but a house just happens to come on the market at a price they can afford.

But before the road trip, there is the walk-through with the real estate agent. Here the family is at their most hopeful, and the real estate agent their most shady. This is the house that has been on the market for far too long, the house that none of the agents have been able to unload, and the asking price is always suspiciously low. Sometimes there's a hint that there is something terribly wrong with the place, that something very bad once happened there: a suggestive frown from the agent when the family isn't looking, a guilty glance around the room when the papers are signed.

Then, of course, there's moving day. The boxes are unloaded, the kids run inside to claim which room will be theirs, while the family dog refuses to cross the threshold and is left barking on the front porch. New places are found for old mementoes, family photos are hung on the wall, and plates and cutlery are unwrapped for the first meal of Chinese take-out. This is when the new owners start to claim the space, to take it over, and begin the process of making the house into their home. As they get acquainted with their new space, a strange stain on the wall they never noticed causes some concern, a hidden room missing from the floorplans is found, Mom and/or Dad start acting strangely. It's when the ghosts begin to stir, sensing that someone has invaded their territory.

When people ask what makes a house a home, the answer is typically "people," but there's more to it than that. There are certain criteria that define the meaning of "home."[7] First and foremost, the home represents security and control (and in some respect, maybe a person's only place of security and control). It's a place of refuge from the outside world. In our home, we control who is allowed access, and we dictate what happens inside. Our home is a reflection of our ideas and values; it's how we want to be seen by others and an expression of our tastes and interests: the books on the coffee table, the style of furniture, the pictures on the wall. The new homeowner hasn't made their mark yet. The boxes are still being unpacked. They're still figuring out where to hang the crucifix. There are none of what Judith Sixsmith calls "contextual markers" in place yet. Another familiar scene in horror involves finding the things the previous owners left behind: the photo album, the music box, the wardrobe, or the dollhouse. These are the material representations of the dead left behind, occupying the space, the physical remnants of the life that was there before.

The home represents the continuity of a life. The transformation of a house into a home is a temporal process that happens over weeks, months, or even years as you "settle in" to a place. The new homeowner has no history in the house and is stepping into someone else's experience. They are picking up another family's story where it left off, and in the case of horror movies, they are inheriting someone else's trauma.

Finally, homes provide privacy, and this is what is most

disturbing to me, the idea that freaks me out the most. A ghost is the ultimate invasion of privacy. The ghost can see us, but we can't see it. It watches us while we're sleeping; it hides under our bed and in the closet. It writes messages on our bathroom mirror while we're in the shower and pulls the sheets off us while we sleep. It spies on us when we're most vulnerable, when we are the most naked in every possible way. In the haunted house, we are being watched all the time. A house that is haunted is a house under constant surveillance.

The home serves as a proxy for the people that inhabit it. Our homes are an extension of ourselves, our "physical reference point" outside of our own bodies.[8] When a haunting occurs, the home is no longer a private sanctuary, a place of safety and security. It can't be trusted. It's no longer ours. The uncanny (or unheimlich), according to Freud, is the phenomenon of something that was once familiar and intimate becoming strange and exposed. That warm and cozy feeling, that "sense of peaceful pleasure and security as in one within the four walls of his house," disappears, and is replaced by something alien. The un-home. In the haunted home we watch powerlessly as something we once knew intimately turns unrecognizable and impossible. When the kitchen chairs start assembling themselves, when doors open on their own, when the crucifix on the wall turns upside-down, our home reverts to its unfamiliar state before it was claimed; it turns back into a house.

What's the Catch?

"There's nothing like it on the market. Not at this price."
— *The Amityville Horror*, 1979

In Lewis Allen's *The Uninvited* (1944), Roderick Fitzgerald

(Ray Milland) and his sister Pamela (Ruth Hussey) stumble across an abandoned mansion by the sea while on vacation in Cornwall. After a few minutes of exploration, they spontaneously decide to buy it then and there. Commander Beech, the owner of Windward House, offers it to the siblings for well below its worth, but asks Pamela if she wouldn't be nervous in such a lonely house: "The wind at night, it plays odd tricks in old houses."

"Are you trying to tell us the house is haunted?" She asks teasingly.

In all seriousness, Beech replies, "No, Miss Fitzgerald, no house is haunted, but I had some tenants five years ago who complained of [*dramatic pause*] disturbances." Roderick counters that a story like that should bring the price of the house down, but concedes in the end, and the deal is struck before they can finish their sherry.

With a nervous and slightly bewildered laugh, Roderick says, "Well, it's wonderfully simple to buy a house, isn't it?" For most of us, it's a little more complex and requires more than a handshake and a gentleman's agreement to buy a mansion, but this is a recurring theme in haunted house movies: they're getting a good deal on a big house because something horrible happened there.

In Scott Derrickson's *Sinister* (2012), true-crime author Ellison Oswalt (Ethan Hawke) moves his wife and children into a house where the events of his latest project took place. Unlike for Roderick and Pamela, the choice to buy the house places a significant financial burden on his family. Their old house hasn't sold, so they're losing money paying two mortgages. They're dependent on this new, yet-to-be-written book becoming a bestseller so they can get out of debt and buy a bigger, undefiled house. They're stuck. Knowing she'd say no to living in yet another place with a grisly history, Ellison withholds the details from his wife. After their son starts having night terrors and their daughter declares that she has been seeing the ghost of a girl, he comes clean to his wife, and the inevitable fight ensues. She is furious he's put his writing before her safety and that of the children. She hasn't experienced anything supernatural, but nonetheless, she's haunted by the house's reputation.

The refreshing thing about *The Amityville Horror* is that Kathy and George know what they're getting into from the start. There isn't that moment of discovery or revelation. There's no trip to the library to sift through microfiche of newspaper articles or to the town historical society to pore over old land surveys (however much I love those scenes), nor is there a foreboding anecdote from an old-timer neighbor who's watched owners come and go over the years. The Lutzes are informed, and the audience is too. The film starts with the showing. However, as the real estate agent takes them through the house, the scene is punctuated with sharp cuts of flashbacks of the murders, and as she extols the benefits and potential of each room, we see flashes of bloody bodies and the blast of a shotgun. Even with the house below market rate at $80,000, the Lutzes are a bit hesitant. They aren't wealthy: George has his own small contracting business he works hard to keep afloat. Kathy is a stay-at-home mom. They weigh the pros and cons, one of the cons being that the year before, Ron DeFeo Jr. killed his family as they slept in their beds. Kathy asks George if it bothers him that a family was murdered in the house they are about to buy. "Well, sure," he says. "But houses don't have memories." George will soon come to realize that houses do indeed remember.

In real estate, disclosure documents provide details about

properties that might negatively affect their value. Normally it's banal things like structural damage and property line disputes, but they may also include any deaths that have occurred in the home. However, some deaths are worse than others. Dad's heart attack doesn't have the same punch as familicide. Some states put qualifications on the nature of those deaths and impose a duty to disclose a "stigmatized property." Unlike grandma passing away in her sleep, or an accidental slip and fall from a ladder, a stigmatized death is either a suicide or a murder. The pall of terror or despair from a violent and unexpected demise lingers so heavily over a house that it permanently stains the very structure of the building. Our beliefs and fears about what happens to us when we die, and depending on *how* we died, are significant enough that a so-called "psychologically affected property" can keep buyers away regardless of whether they believe in ghosts or not.[9]

In this Scooby-Doo scenario, ghosts can lower property value, and our existential fears can slip into litigation. In 1991, the New York Supreme Court declared a house legally haunted in the case of *Stambovsky v. Ackley*,[10] commonly known as "The Ghostbusters Ruling" (really). Helen Ackley sold her house to Jeffrey Stambovsky without informing him of its notoriety: "Plaintiff, to his horror, discovered that the house he had recently contracted to purchase was widely reputed to be possessed by poltergeists, reportedly seen by defendant seller and members of her family on numerous occasions over the last nine years."

While in escrow, Stambovsky discovered that his potential home was a popular destination for ghost-hunting tourists and that Ackley herself had advertised the house in the past as "a riverfront Victorian (with ghost)." He wanted to back out and get his down payment back, but she refused. Stambovsky took her to court and won. A quote from the ruling states: "In his pursuit of a legal remedy for fraudulent misrepresentation against the seller, the plaintiff hasn't a ghost of a chance, I am nevertheless moved by the spirit of equity to allow the buyer to seek rescission of the contract of sale and recovery of his down payment." It was a case of proving, not the existence of ghosts, but that the house had a reputation for being haunted, and that was bad enough.

This isn't a new conceit. The first documented instance of supernatural real estate fraud can be found around 100 CE, when scholar, author, lawyer, and prolific epistolarian Pliny the Younger wrote a letter to his friend asking for his thoughts on ghosts.[11] Pliny was told a story about a philosopher named Athenodorus, who purchased a large, roomy house in Athens despite its notoriety as an "ill-reputed and pestilential house." The "extraordinary cheapness raised his suspicion," but it was too good of a deal to resist. Besides, Athenodorus was an intelligent, rational man who didn't believe in ghosts. But after a visit from a beaconing apparition, moaning and clacking chains, he changed his tune.

The timelessness of this scenario is telling. This conflict of finance over fear is a battle for the ages. A house is likely the most valuable asset a person has. Because of this, it's also the most significant financial burden one is likely to face, with all the emotions, fears, and worries that come with it. In most horror movies, the houses are often larger, grander, and more impressive than the family could normally afford, and they present a tantalizing offer of upward mobility: the bigger house, the higher salary, the better life. These houses are symbolic of having *almost* made it. It is the cruelest of optimism: they nearly had it, they almost got what they'd been dreaming of, but then something beyond their control says, "Not so fast. This house is ours."

There is an epilogue at the end of *Amityville* after the Lutzes drive off into the night, which states that they never returned to reclaim their house or their personal belongings. The Lutzes aren't wealthy, but they were comfortable enough to make the decision to put their family's safety ahead of financial loss and abandon the property they'd just bought and everything in it. This is indicative of the level of terror and trauma they experienced. Despite their financial troubles, the idea of going back into the house to reclaim all their worldly possessions and valuables was worse. But not everyone has that option. The real Lutz family sent movers back to retrieve their furniture.

Freedom is a big part of the American Dream, including freedom of mobility: the ability to go where the jobs are, to move to a new city or state to follow opportunities, to leave where you are and go somewhere else if you want to. Even the phrase "upward mobility" suggests relocation. The pursuit of happiness means you get to go wherever you might be happy, to do what is best for your interests. We saw it in the Great Migrations of Black people from the agricultural South to the industrial North and in the waves of immigrants past and present in search of a better life. Manifest destiny told us to "go west, young man," but this part of the American ideology is in direct contradiction with the long-term mortgage that locks you not only to a city or state but to a specific property for decades.

In James Wan's *The Conjuring* (2013), the Perron family's situation is similar to that of the Lutz family, and like *The Amityville Horror*, is roughly (very, very roughly) based on a true story. Carolyn and Roger Perron (Lili Taylor and Ron Livingston) have a large family of five daughters. Carolyn is a stay-at-home mom and Roger is a truck driver whose employment is precarious. Financially, they're getting by. They bought their house at auction with no knowledge of the previous owner (no disclosure agreement).

After going through all sorts of supernatural terrors, paranormal investigator Ed Warren (Patrick Wilson) asks them why they don't just move out. Roger says, "I don't know where we would move to. We got all our money tied up into this place, plus all the repairs on top of that. I don't know anybody who would take in a family of seven indefinitely."

Before the Federal Housing Administration (FHA) and New Deal programs in the 1930s, mortgage repayment periods generally averaged less than ten years. The FHA doubled this, and smaller down payments meant more people could buy homes, but with longer mortgages. This wasn't just an economic plan to stabilize the housing market: Roosevelt wanted to frame citizenship based on homeownership. Nineteenth-century political economist Willard Phillips reasoned that homeownership gave individuals a stake in society, and that if a citizen felt invested in the economy, they'd be less likely to question it, and less likely to look upon it as

> *an inhabitant of a conquered territory looks upon a citadel of the conqueror. Give him hope, give him the chances of providing for his family, of laying up a store for his old age, of commanding some cheap comfort or luxury, upon which he sets his heart; and he will voluntarily and cheerfully submit to privations and hardships.* "[12]

The mortgage is an illusion of stability, and if the subprime housing crisis of 2008 is any indication, it's one that is powerful enough to bring ruin to the wishful thinkers and threaten to upend the whole economic system. In the haunted house, as with many of the indignities of capitalism and the neoliberal agenda, what is considered a sign of independence becomes a trap in the face of supernatural forces. In *Sinister, The Amityville Horror, The Conjuring,* and *The Haunting in Connecticut,* the financial burden is established from the beginning. In *Poltergeist,* the horror is in the invasion of the comfort and calm of a stable home. But in these other films, economic dread lays a foundation for worse things to come. The horror is driven by the lack of options, and unlike the Lutzes, not everyone can just leave. You can either stay, resign yourself to supernatural occupation, and hope the Warrens take your case, or you surrender and flee.

Peter Cornwell's *The Haunting in Connecticut* (2009) combines the stresses of homeownership and the general crappiness of the American healthcare system. The film opens with an interview with Sara Campbell (Virginia Madsen), telling her story to a reporter. "I moved into the house because it's what we so desperately needed at that time." We know from the start that her family are vulnerable and desperate. Sara has been driving her son Matt (Kyle Gallner) back and forth to the hospital, where he has been receiving an experimental cancer treatment. It's an eight-hour drive. He's weak and sick, and Sara's exhausted. Her husband, Peter (Martin Donovan), has put all their money into his business, their son's medication is extremely expensive, and they've taken in a few extended family members, so there are more mouths to feed. It's clear that the situation is unsustainable, so they decide to bite the bullet and rent a place closer to the hospital, even if it means paying rent on top of a mortgage.

While looking for a place, Sara drives by a man hammering a "for rent" sign in front of a house, who jokes, "I'll give you the first month free if I don't have to finish hammering this darn sign." As he takes her on a tour of the house, she says, "It's perfect. It's everything we need. It's spacious and affordable. I'm just wondering, where's the catch?"

He answers, "Well, it does have a bit of a history…" It turns out the house was a former funeral home — a bit creepy perhaps — but she and Peter assure the kids that there's nothing to worry about, it's just a house. Later they discover that the original owner was a necromancer who raised a horde of the undead to do his evil bidding; Matt becomes the focus of torment and is possessed by the spirit of the mortician's young medium.

As Matt's behavior gets stranger and stranger, Peter becomes increasingly stressed about their financial situation. He comes home drunk one night, furious that all the lights are on, shouting, "Why don't we just build a fire and throw money into it!" smashing lightbulbs and telling them they can sleep in the dark. The family huddles together in fear, not of a ghost or a demon, but of their enraged and resentful father. They are already living in a bit of a horror story, and an armoire full of corpses with missing eyelids is just unnecessarily cruel.

This scenario often reoccurs in horror films, where domestic strain adds to the tension. There are dual layers of dread: the unknown paranormal force that terrorizes the family, and the known stress of a financial burden put on the father/husband. To quote Berlant: "For the bourgeois there is property, there is home, and the man is a little leader in the home, and everyone recognizes his authority wherever he carries his propriety onto property."

In *Amityville*, George takes a break from the chaos of home to have a drink with his business partner. As he's fallen deeper under the influence of the house, George has been neglecting his work, and his partner tells him: "I told you you were taking on too much. You marry a dame with three kids, you buy a big house with mortgages up to your ass, you change your religion, and you forget about business." The scene is similar to the "White Man's Burden" conversation Jack has in *The Shining*. When a bottle of bourbon materializes just in time, Jack complains to his ghostly bartender that his ungrateful and unforgiving wife doesn't appreciate the heavy weight of the responsibilities he bears to his employer.

In the horror genre, there's usually a strict adherence to patriarchal norms; the man's role is to protect and provide for his family, and his impotence in both areas leaves him angry and sometimes volatile. The ghosts become the authority, and Dad is left with little to do but drink whiskey all day and wield baseball bats at night. With the authority snatched away from the living, the question becomes: Whose house is this anyway?

This House is Ours

"I have heard myself say that a house with a death in it can never again be bought or sold by the living. It can only be borrowed from the ghosts that have stayed behind."
— *I Am the Pretty Thing That Lives in the House,* (2016)

Who can claim ownership of a haunted house: the living who just moved in or the dead who never left? Who is doing the haunting, and who is being haunted? In Alejandro Amenábar's *The Others* (2001), a large manor house in the Channel Islands stands isolated in a sea of perpetual fog. Having been occupied by the Nazis during the war, the house is back in the hands of its rightful owners, but who the rightful owners *are* remains to be seen. The current residents,

Grace Stewart (Nicole Kidman) and her children, Anne and Nicholas (Alakina Mann and James Bentley), are alone in the house since her husband has still not returned from the war and the servants have mysteriously disappeared. In addition to this melancholic atmosphere, Anne and Nicholas suffer from an extreme photosensitive condition such that any bit of sunlight causes them extreme pain. Curtains are always kept tightly shut and doors are kept locked for their own protection, and with little natural light, much of the house is left in darkness, with no illumination stronger than that from an oil lamp. But just when Grace needs them, housekeeper Mrs Bertha Mills (Fionnula Flanagan), gardener Edmund Tuttle (Eric Sykes), and a mute girl named Lydia (Elaine Cassidy) arrive unannounced at Grace's door seeking employment. Conveniently, they used to work in that very house. But soon after the "new" servants arrive, strange things start to happen; curtains are drawn without anyone having touched them, locked doors are left wide open. For Grace, these simple gestures are malevolent acts of violence by an intruder set on harming her children.

There are multiple owners of this house, each from different moments in time, in different states of being, and each claiming a right to be there. There are the servants, the Old Ghosts, the ones who have been dead the longest and know that they're dead. They know the house, and they know their place in its uncanny social structure. There are the current residents, Grace, and her children: these are the New Ghosts, and they don't yet know that they're dead. As the protagonists, we, like them, assume that they are the ones being haunted, that they are the ones being invaded. But then there are the new owners, the Living, who have just moved in and simply want to keep the curtains open and the doors unlocked. It's Grace and her children who are the ghosts wreaking havoc and terrorizing an innocent family. They are the things that go bump in the night.

Each group is experiencing an invasion of privacy, that disruption of predictable comfort we associate with the home, but in different ways. Mrs Mills becomes a mentor for Grace, helping her get accustomed to her condition. Grace becomes the staunch, lingering spirit who refuses to give up her home in stubborn rebellion. The Living have had enough, say forget it, and just move out. Score one for the New Ghosts.

His House, Regency Enterprises / Album/ Alamy Stock Photo

Questions of identity and autonomy, of control and stability, of options and mobility, plus the idea of homeownership being proof of nationality and true citizenship, are not the purview of the United States alone. Remi Weekes' *His House* (2020) does not take place in America, but it *is* about a dream. Like many of these movies, *His House* is about a couple moving to a new place to get a fresh start and carrying the baggage of unresolved issues with them. The husband, burdened by the need to provide for his family, becomes angry and resentful of his inability to do so as their dreams are dashed by a malignant supernatural force.

But in *His House*, the couple's journey does not start with a hopeful car ride to the suburbs, but with a desperate escape from an impending massacre. Bol (Sope Dirisu) and Rial (Wunmi Mosaku) are refugees fleeing war-torn South Sudan. Rial has made it onto an overcrowded bus, but the doors close on Bol, the driver only allowing children. In a panic, he grabs a seemingly abandoned child and pretends to be her father, ensuring himself a seat. But the girl was not abandoned, and as the bus drives away, her mother runs behind, screaming for her child, the girl crying for her mother. Rial promises the child that she will take care of her, but while crossing the English Channel, their raft capsizes and many of the refugees drown, including the little girl.

But Bol and Rial survive, and after three months in a detention center, they are finally assigned a house in the outskirts of London. The neighborhood resembles most government housing — rows of cinder-block, terraced houses that all look the same — but they are finally safe, free, and alive. The house is not much, but it's theirs. Sort of. As asylum seekers, they are told they must adhere to strict rules about what they can and cannot do or they'll risk being returned to detention and possibly back to South Sudan, two of those rules being that they must reside in a house of the board's choosing and are not allowed to move.

Homeownership for Bol and Rial is dictated by stringent regulations, so their grasp on security, safety, and control is tentative. They also soon learn that the claim to their home is not only contingent on adhering to the rules but on conforming to and blending into the culture. The case agent reiterates over and over that the house is all theirs, it is *their* house. He tells them they'll be all right as long as they fit in, and to "make it easy for people. Be one of the good ones." Their claim of ownership is conditional on their ability to assimilate into British culture, in effect to become British. So if the home is an extension of the self, they are being told they must reject who they are to conform to the house, not the other way around.

Soon after they move in, Bol is tormented by multiple gruesome apparitions and becomes increasingly unhinged. He hammers holes through the walls in an attempt to get at the creatures hidden inside, shouting with fury, "This is *my* house! *My* house." But in the very next scene, he's sitting in the case agent's office, submissive and deferential, trying to convince the agent to give them another house. It's not his house and never was.

Bol's method of dealing with this terror is to forget, to assimilate, to become the house they have now, not the home they left behind. He buys new clothes, hangs out at the local pub, and insists that when they eat, they sit at the table and use cutlery instead of on the floor with their fingers as they would in Sudan. He lives in a state of guilt-ridden denial, determined to assert his right to his home despite the efforts of both the ghosts and the government.

Rial knows what these ghosts are and why they are here. Rial believes they were sent there by an apeth (a night witch). She tells Bol a story about a good but poor man who wanted so badly to have a house of his own that he stole money from an old man. That old man turned out to be a witch who sent a demon to the man's house to torment him. Rial believes an apeth followed them from Sudan to England as punishment for taking what was not theirs, the little girl.

She listens to the spirits and talks to them, and unlike Bol, she resists assimilation and wants to remember and keep part of her homeland with her. As Gaston Bachelard writes, "Not only our memories, but the things we have forgotten are 'housed.' Our soul is an abode."[13] In an effort to gain control of this space, enforce his claim as the owner, and drive out the monsters, Bol burns everything from their past, all of Rial's reminders of their life before England. He is, in effect, attempting to erase her memories of her old home to get her to accept the new house — or perhaps to get the house to accept *her*. Rial, like most of us, needs to claim space by marking the home with relics of the past, the materiality of memory. Bol denies this of Rial, making it impossible for the house ever truly to be theirs. But it never truly was theirs to begin with.

At the end of *The Others*, Grace leads her children in a chant of "this house is ours, this house is ours," as they watch the living family abandon the house they just bought, like the Oswalt family in *Sinister* or the Lutz family in *The Amityville Horror*. In *The Conjuring* and *A Haunting in Connecticut*, the ghosts are exorcised, the houses are cleaned, and the family is once again safe in their home. Usually, either the ghosts leave or the people do. At the end of *His House*, Bol and Rial's home is packed with the ghosts of refugees, not only from their boat but from all over the world. The couple stands with them side by side, as they easily could have been among them. They patch the holes, paint the walls, and stay where they are, choosing to acknowledge the dead and live among them in their new home.

There have been ghost stories as long as there have been

people, and I imagine there have been haunted house stories as long as there have been houses. But there is a particular theme of property rights and homeownership in gothic literature that goes back to the first gothic novel, Horace Walpole's *The Castle of Otranto,* written in 1794. In the story, Manfred, the lord of the castle of Otranto, is haunted by an ominous, somewhat cryptic prophecy: "...that the castle and lordship of Otranto should pass from the present family, whenever the real owner should be grown too large to inhabit it." He's about to marry off his only son and heir, Conrad, but he's crushed to death by a gigantic helmet on his wedding day. To secure his place as the lord of the castle, Manfred tries to force Isabella (the woman betrothed to his son) to marry *him*. All sorts of confusing shenanigans ensue, but the question of who has a right to the property, and who can claim ownership, drives the narrative and threads through every haunted house story since. Who does the house belong to, the family that just moved in or the dead who never left? The core of the haunted house story is that tension, that shift in control between the living with the deed and the ghosts who don't care.

The real Butch DeFeo never came clean about why he killed his family, but he did say, "There was no demon. You know who the demon is? I'm the demon."[14] He said he heard voices, that he was suffering from a paranoid delusion that his family were planning on killing him. He was also doing a lot of heroin at the time. Ronald Sr was controlling, abusive, and volatile toward his family, and may or may not have had ties to the mob. George Lutz was also a controlling, volatile, father, who (according to Kathy's son Christopher Quaratino) greatly exaggerated any paranormal activity there may have been.[15] No one really knows what really happened to the Lutzes in those twenty-eight days, but it is true that George and Kathy Lutz knew about the DeFeo murders and bought the house anyway for just $80,000 (just like in the movie). George showed their friends the bullet holes in the bedroom walls, and they kept some of the furniture, including the frame of the bed where Dawn DeFeo was found face down with a gunshot to the head like the rest of her family. Kathy thought the house was charming and the kids didn't care about its sordid past. George thought, "It was a dream come true."[16]

The dream of homeownership is less about the house than about what a house means: security, autonomy, the guarantee of shelter in which to protect our loved ones from the elements and those that mean us harm. It means a family, a household. Nine years before the murders, the DeFeo family moved from a small apartment in Brooklyn to a three-story house in a quaint Long Island town with a pool and a boathouse. It was their dream too. When they moved in, Ronald Sr put a sign on the front lawn that said "High Hopes" in big black letters, and during their brief residence in the house on Ocean Avenue, the Lutzes kept it there.

Brutal Houses

Evil Lairs & Party Houses

"If I wanted to build a nice, cozy, unpretentious insane asylum, he'd be the man for it."

— *The Black Cat* (1934)

It is a dark and stormy night. A pair of travelers, stranded on a road in an unfamiliar country, look up desperately at their only option for shelter, a foreboding mansion perched high on the top of a hill. We are in Eastern Europe, some remote area between Budapest and Visegrád in Hungary. But unlike the medieval spires of a ruined castle, this house is a modern construction with clean horizontal planes dotted with glowing rectangles of light from the windows. It's a classic horror introduction with a modern silhouette.

The house belongs to Hjalmar Poelzig (Boris Karloff), a former Austro-Hungarian WWI commander turned architect,[1] in the 1934 film *The Black Cat*, directed by Edgar G. Ulmer. On the way to their honeymoon, American novelist Peter Alison (David Manners) and his wife Joan (Jacqueline Wells) share a ride with Dr. Vitus Werdegast (Béla Lugosi), who is on his way to visit his "old friend" Poelzig. Werdegast has been in a Russian prison camp for the past fifteen years and, unbeknownst to the newlyweds, is on his way to Poelzig to seek revenge for betraying him in the war (and also for stealing his wife and daughter).

Inside, the space is vast and open, a house of glass-brick walls, unadorned spaces, and gleaming Art Deco furnishings, not a single cobweb or dust-covered sculpture from antiquity in sight. When asked to picture a haunted house, we typically imagine an imposing, overly ornate Victorian in decay. Rarely do we equate minimalism with haunted houses.

The Black Cat (1934), Edgar G. Ulmer

Alison surveys his surroundings with a bemused discomfort, sensing something a bit off in the gleaming veneer. He says, "This is a very interesting house you have here. It has an atmosphere..." Werdegast interrupts, "An atmosphere of death." While it may be modern, nothing is ever entirely new. Like in all houses of horror, there is something hidden in the basement, something soaked in the land and embedded in the earth below it. As Edwin Heathcote writes, "There is no such thing as a fresh start in architecture."[2] The house was built from the very ruins of Fort Marmorus, where the traitorous Commander Poelzig gave up his troops' location to the Russians, leaving thousands of soldiers to die in a bloody battle. Poelzig decided to build his gleaming house right on top of the scene of his crime.

Aside from Werdegast's ailurophobia (fear of cats), the film carries little resemblance to the titular story by Edgar Allan Poe — except for the presence of a hidden, dead wife. In the basement, in the remnants of the former gun turrets, is his collection of dead women. They're dressed in white gowns and suspended inside upright glass caskets, perfectly preserved with their pencil-thin eyebrows and finger waves intact. Werdegast's wife is among them, on display next to the grid of a massive firing range chart, like a specimen in a laboratory. Unlike Poe's narrator, Poelzig doesn't seem particularly guilty about what he's done.

The Black Cat was made between the wars. Released in the United States just a year after Hitler came to power, it's a study of the remnants of the First World War while the second one is just on the horizon. If WWI was a technologically modern kind of war, Poelzig's house was an architecturally modern house of horrors. The controlled and clean sterility of the house is antithetical to the chaos of the war and his own personal atrocities. The gleaming floors above can't completely conceal the bullet-ridden stone walls below. Underneath Poelzig's severely pointed and gleaming pompadour, the trauma he and Werdegast endured lingers, and rather than deny it, he chose to live on top of it, as either an audacious trophy or a penance, I'm not sure which. Poelzig tells Werdegast, "You say your soul was killed and that you have been dead all these years. And what of me? Did we not both die here at Marmorus fifteen years ago. Are we not both the living dead?"

The Black Cat signifies a shift in the architecture of horror. In the dusty decay of Victorian mansions or abandoned farmhouses, the dead are with us in every old picture frame, the passing of time evident in creaking floorboards and corners draped with spiderwebs. Mortality is blatantly material. In the modern lair, the rot is all internal, the decay repressed, with the concrete poured on top sealing it inside. Its glass walls are deceptively transparent; cantilevered living rooms hang precipitously over cliffs; and its minimal sleekness is suspiciously pristine. Rather than the gothic family houses falling like Usher, the modernist house of horror signals capitalist greed and the corruptive power of wealth. These are homes for Tony Stark or Jeff Bezos. Ghosts of the dead haunt houses with creaky floors and dusty attics. In the modern mansion, the living are the ones who do the terrorizing.

There is a similar architectural approach to the opening of William Castle's camp classic *House on Haunted Hill* (1959). The film begins with the sounds of a woman's screams, ghostly moans, and clanking chains, before a disembodied head emerges from the darkness. Like in *The Black Cat*, the shape against the night sky is not a series of vertical turrets, pitched gables, and arched windows. The house behind Vincent Price's disembodied head is a structure of horizontal trapezoids comprising concrete blocks embossed in geometric patterns. It's closer to a Mesoamerican temple than a Victorian manor.

House on Haunted Hill, Allied Artists (1959)

Unlike in *The Black Cat*, the interior fails to follow through, and reverts to what we expect of a haunted house: candelabras in the foyer, baroque carved mirrors and picture frames, classical statues, and paneled wood doors. It is a mélange of eras and places: a modern house in California that looks like a Mayan temple from two thousand years ago on the outside, with a British Victorian interior. But as the guests tour the exterior of this strange place while the opening credits roll, anticipation is set for an unusual evening. The uncanny architecture prepares us for something strange, even sinister inside. Based on the exterior, it's difficult to imagine what could be happening on the inside.

Millionaire Frederick Loren (Vincent Price) is throwing a "haunted house" themed birthday party for his fourth wife, whom he gleefully despises. Annabelle (Carol Ohmart) is equally disgusted by her husband, and the two volley cruel witticisms back and forth like it's an old game they've played for years. "You remember the fun we had when you poisoned me?" he asks her. According to the party rules, each guest will be rewarded $10,000 if they stay and survive the night in the house. The doors are locked at midnight and the windows are barred. The fortress-like exterior amplifies the impression that once you go in, you may never come out. Spooky shenanigans ensue.

Castle's choice to use Frank Lloyd Wright's Ennis House is an interesting one, breaking away from the traditional architecture horror movie audiences were accustomed to. He's not the only director to take advantage of its dramatic architecture. The pattern of interlocking squares in the concrete blocks resemble circuit boards in Ridley Scott's *Blade Runner* (1982), and perhaps because of its tomb-like quality, Joss Whedon used it for Angel, Spike, and Drucilla's house in *Buffy the Vampire Slayer*.

Frank Lloyd Wright designed the house for Charles and Mabel Ennis in 1924, and it's the largest of the five concrete block, Mayan revival houses Wright designed in Los Angeles. Even more imposing is the John Sowden House, designed by his son Lloyd Wright. Commissioned by John and Ruth Sowden as a party house in 1926, Lloyd Wright's interpretation of his father's style is pushed to a theatrical degree. Nicknamed "The Jaws House," the façade features a glass wall framed top and bottom with blocks formed like ziggurats. It resembles a monstrous open mouth with concrete teeth prepared to chomp down on whoever dares approach.

The most famous images of the house show it nearly engulfed with trees and plants as if one could walk up the steps from Franklin Avenue in Los Feliz and into a Central American jungle. The doorway is flanked by flat windowless concrete surface, a massive wall, and the only way inside is through the jaws. The interior of the house is focused on a central courtyard, where John and Ruth would entertain their artist friends and host performances around the pool. The design is suitably dramatic. The house looks intriguing but secretive, a place meant either for ancient rituals and sacred ceremonies or drug-fueled orgies with movie executives and art dealers. Or both.

Snowden House, Lloyd Wright, 1940 / Historical American Buildings Survey, Library of Congress

But the house would become infamous for reasons other than its fantastical architecture. In 1945 it was bought by Dr George Hodel, who would become the prime suspect in the still-unsolved grisly murder of Elizabeth Short, also known as the Black Dahlia. The 2019 limited television series *I Am the Night* is based on the memoir of Fauna Hodel, George's granddaughter. It focuses on the investigation into Hodel and was filmed on-location in the actual house. Jefferson Mayes, who plays Hodel, said, "You go in and you're sort of sucked up this esophagus of an entrance, a lightless hallway scourged into the central courtyard, and all the rooms are arranged around the courtyard like cells. I felt like I was in a penitentiary, one of those 18th-century panopticons. It's the house of a control freak, and it's a super villain's lair." India Eisley, who plays Fauna, said, "It has a very, very heavy energy there. It's just so isolated, it feels like a mausoleum. You could imagine someone screaming in there and not being heard."[3]

Although cadaver dogs supposedly found evidence that someone died in there at some point, it was never proven definitively that George Hodel killed Elizabeth Short at the Sowden House or elsewhere. But he was guilty of doing some very bad things on the other side of those concrete teeth, somewhere in the guts of the house, and he remains the prime suspect, even after his death. With a house that looks as if it was designed for debauchery, nefarious activity seems inevitable. Death and tragedy, both fictional and real, hover over these Wright houses in Los Angeles, so far away from the peace of the prairie.

In 1911, Wright built a house and studio for himself and his lover Martha "Mamah" Borthwick Cheney in Spring Green, Wisconsin. Wright was married with six kids at the time, and Martha was married to his client Edwin Cheney. The Cheneys divorced, the Wrights did not. The questionable marital situation of this unconventional architect was the source of much gossip in Wisconsin. A *Fort Wayne Sentinel* article from 1914 with the headline "Take Queer View of Marital Life" noted that "everybody directly concerned in this drama seems to be content with things as they are."[4] The article quotes Wright linking his philosophy of architecture with a philosophy of life: "Forms are not sacred. The spirit alone is. There is one thing of greater importance than the home of yesterday, and that is the home of tomorrow."

He called the house Taliesin, and it would become the site of one of the largest mass murders in Wisconsin history. On Saturday, 15 August, 1914, while Wright was away working in Chicago, butler/handyman Julian Carlton served lunch to Mamah and her children, twelve-year-old John and eight-year-old Martha, then split their heads open with a hatchet. He then went to the other side of the house, where the workers and draftsmen were waiting for their lunch, locked them in the room, and poured gasoline under the door. He struck a match setting the house, and those trapped inside, on fire. Seven people in total were killed.

Carlton attempted suicide by drinking muriatic acid but was apprehended still alive. Little is known about Carlton and his wife, Gertrude, who worked as the cook. They came from Chicago or Alabama or Barbados or Cuba; it's still not known which for sure. There has never been a motive revealed for why he did it other than "insanity." Maybe Wright was about to fire him; maybe he owed Carlton money. Back in Chicago he was known to be sometimes volatile, erratic, and paranoid. We will never know his motives because Carlton, with his throat so badly burned by the acid, died of starvation eight weeks after his capture.

Six months after the murders, still grieving and with his career stagnating, Wright left the Midwest behind and, like so many people then and now, moved to Los Angeles to reinvent himself. While visiting the Panama California Exposition in San Diego, he was taken by drawings of pre-Columbian temples and inspired to create a "truly American" form of architecture (if "American" means profiting off the appropriation of indigenous cultures). While we can't draw a direct line from Taliesin to Wright's work in Los Angeles, it is notable that the inspiration for the houses he made after the murders came from structures designed to honor the dead. The Ennis House is complex, strange, imposing; it's a house that "seems to repel the very idea of normal family life."[5] While it may be more *Blade Runner* than *Brady Bunch*, the house was a home. Hodel's son Steven (a former LAPD homicide detective, convinced his father is indeed the Black Dahlia murder) wrote about growing up in the Sowden House, "It was like entering a cave with secret stone tunnels, within which only the initiated could feel comfortable."[6] Frank Lloyd Wright biographer Brendan Gill said Wright's Los Angeles houses "are better suited to sheltering a Mayan god than an American family." But who is to say what constitutes an "American family" and what an American house should look like. The Sowden House, like many modernist houses, may not be the image we think of when we think of a family home, but that depends on the family. Steve Hodel's memories of this house paint a different picture:

> *My brothers and I saw it as a place of magic that we were convinced could easily have greeted the uninvited with pits of fire, poison darts, deadly snakes. From any room one could step into a central courtyard full of exotic foliage and beautiful giant cactus plants reaching straight into the sky. Once inside this remarkable house*

one found oneself in absolute privacy, invisible to the outside world.[7]

Whatever Wright was working through in Los Angeles, his goal was to fundamentally alter the way we build houses and how we live inside them. Regarding Taliesin, the *Fort Wayne Sentinel* went on to say that along with his house, "Mr Wright says there is something else building — character, artistic ideals, unfettered selfhood, spiritual communion, sweetness, fidelity to the higher code and a broader service to humanity."[8] It's a lofty goal for a building that, despite its intention, did not inspire sweetness or spiritual communion from Julian Carlton. Design can only get you so far.

Machines for Living

"Ever wanted something more? Ever thought there could be a better way to live free from the shackles of the old, tired world? So why not join us?"

— promotional trailer for *High-Rise* (2019)

The Ennis house rises from a platform on multiple levels made of 27,000 textured and perforated concrete blocks embossed with a Greek key design. The use of concrete in home construction was still new in 1924, but Wright and his peers — among them Mies Van Der Rohe, Paul Rudolph, and Erno Goldfinger[9] — saw its potential for use in affordable housing. Concrete was inexpensive, made on-site, and could be molded into anything. Wright said, "It was the cheapest (and ugliest) thing in the building world. Why not see what could be done with that gutter rat? It might be permanent, noble beautiful."[10]

After the decimation of WWII across England and Europe, the need for housing was particularly urgent, and concrete became the miracle building material. It's still the number one building material in the world by a long shot. Concrete is a humble workhorse of a material, a grey soupy mix of water, cement, and gravel that's inexpensive, available anywhere, and can look like anything. It can be molded into perfectly identical blocks, embossed with designs, and poured into impossible curving shapes or precariously massive cantilevers that seem to defy physics. Along with sprawling, modern homes for the rich, it became the material of government buildings, churches and synagogues, universities and institutions. Concrete was for both billionaire mansions and public housing.

In 1947, French architect Le Corbusier was commissioned to design a multi-unit apartment building in Marseille to house the thousands of citizens displaced by the war. Unable to afford steel, he used raw concrete, or *béton brut*. The term "brutalism" comes from the material, not a critique of its aesthetics. Corbusier's Unité d'Habitation was completed in 1951, with a vision for living that would become a model for public housing around the world. Raw concrete is rough, bare, without ornament or refinement, so there is an inherent severity in the material that lives up to its coincidentally autological name. However, the intent of these buildings was decisively humanist, attempting to change people's lives — and therefore society — for the better. At least that was the idea. Avery Trufelman referred to concrete as an "utterly optimistic building material. Arguably, too optimistic."[11]

Cité Radieuse, Le Corbusier, Dino Fracchia

Corbusier called his building a "vertical city," where its inhabitants could live and play together; a village on stilts, with air conditioning and a rooftop terrace with a swimming pool. The balcony walls were painted in bold, primary colors, turning the cool grey grid into a Mondrian painting. It was designed with Corbusier's Modulor universal measuring unit, based on the height of a six-foot-tall man with his arms raised— even its proportions were based on a human ideal.

But the people of Marseille called it the *maison du fada*, or "house of a madman." It was far away from the city, away from the thriving street life people were used to, an isolated "city within a city." Intended to be a new kind of communal experience, there was shopping on the seventh and eighth floors, a restaurant, a kindergarten, a library, a post office, a gym on the roof, and a restaurant called *Le Ventre de l'Architecte*, or "The Belly of the Architect." In a critique for *Architectural Review* before its opening, architect Kenneth Easton wondered,

"How could 1,600 of this essentially 'agora-minded' and volatile community ever be happily contained in this great rectangle on the outskirts of the town?" Good question.

David Cronenberg's *Shivers* (1975) takes place entirely inside the Starliner Tower apartment building, another city within a city on the outskirts of town. Played by Ludwig Mies van der Rohe's Tourelle-Sur-Rive, it was built in 1962 on Nuns' Island in Montreal. The building is classically modernist in form: horizontal, clean lines; a uniform concrete grid framing glass walls.

The building is isolated on an actual island away from the rest of the city, and it too is at the mercy of a madman. The film begins with a slideshow sales pitch as apartment manager Mr Merrick (Ronald Mlodzik) recites the many benefits of living in this self-contained island paradise. The photos are ironically dismal and banal: an ordinary kitchen, the parking lot, and a depressing view of the St Lawrence River. Amenities include cable tv, modern appliances, a golf course, a swimming pool, a restaurant, a variety store, a deli, a boutique, a drug store, a dry cleaner, and dental and medical clinics (which will come in handy). Merrick exalts that "day-to-day living becomes a luxury cruise when you've made your home at Starliner Tower Apartments!" While it may be only 12.5 minutes from downtown Montreal, its inhabitants might as well be in the middle of the ocean, and the comparison to a cruise ship seems apt considering their notorious reputation for disease outbreaks.

As a young couple applies for an apartment in the lobby office, Dr Emil Hobbes (Fred Doederlein) is violently attacking a young woman in apartment 1511. While the couple considers their options for an apartment with a view, Annabelle Brown lies unconscious and near naked on a dining room table as Hobbes cuts her open with a scalpel and pours acid into her abdomen before slicing his own throat. Hobbes is attempting to stop a disaster that he started. Looking to find an alternative to organ transplants, he has bred a parasite that could take over the job of sickly human organs. But Hobbes' true intent was more sinister, albeit idealistic in his own way. He too wanted to create a better way to live, believing that humans think too much and are too far removed from our basic natural instincts. His parasite is "a combination of aphrodisiac and venereal disease that will hopefully turn the world into one beautiful, mindless orgy."

The gleaming, liver-colored, slug-like creature slithers its way up walls and through garbage chutes throughout the building, passing through its residents one by one, infesting them with an over-powering sex drive resulting in everyone — young and old, gay and straight, Black and white — feverishly going door-to-door in search of victims to molest, culminating in a mass orgy in the Olympic-sized pool. Honestly, it seems pretty fun. In the end, the once-contained parasite, having exhausted its hosts in the Starliner, escapes the confines of the island as the tenants gleefully drive out of the parking garage and cross the bridge into Montreal.

Like *Shivers*, a teaser for Ben Wheatley's 2015 adaptation of J.G. Ballard's novel *High-Rise* takes the form of an advertisement for an apartment building. The narrator lists the many modern amenities the building has to offer, everything you could possibly need or want: "There is almost no reason to leave." These experiments in better living through rebar attempt to expand the border of the home beyond the private space into a community, putting a whole neighborhood under one roof and creating an encapsulated world better than the one outside. Like *Shivers*, the isolated ecosystem of the building creates an ideal breeding ground for the breakdown of society and the degradation of civility into primal chaos. There is no other society than that within the walls of the high-rise. The laws and mores in the world beyond the parking lot no longer apply. The rest of the world might as well not exist.

Isolation may foster either self-sufficiency or dependency, and for the tenants of the high-rise it's the latter. The building becomes the nurturing entity, the means of sustenance, society, and survival. But when the system fails, when resources become slim, and infrastructure breaks down, the home becomes a trap. Practically speaking, the more remote the location, the more vital the amenities become, the more crucial the conveniences, the greater the fidelity to the building and the less likely its tenants are to abandon it when things go wrong.

At first, life seems ordinary enough for Dr Robert Laing (Tom Hiddleston), the building's newest tenant, in his "over-priced cell." He's not an immediate fan of the design. He finds the concrete landscape alienating; architecture designed for war. We'll come to realize how apt that analogy is. Most of the tenants are like him: professional, educated middle-class people living on the middle floors of the building, ever hoping to go a little higher. The families with children are relegated to the lower floors, their noisy and messy lives kept far away from the uber-cool, more affluent tenants on the highest floors. When the social order of the building breaks down, those class structures intensify, and the stratification sharpens between the upper floors and those below them. Like Corbusier's Unité d'Habitation, the tenth floor of the high-rise has a supermarket, a bank, a hair salon, a swimming pool, a gym, an elementary school, and most importantly, a liquor store. There's a second pool on the thirty-fifth floor, a sauna, and a restaurant. "Delighted by this glut of conveniences, Laing made less and less effort to leave the building."[12] In his review of Unité d'Habitation, architect Thurston William worried that "the housewife will have little need and less inclination ever to leave the building at all for days on end." [13]

The film gives us a visual interpretation of the building: a tower rising into the sky with a sudden and unnerving bend at the top; a brutalist specialty: uncanny forms of impossible balance. The top floors of the apartments' ruling class jut out further and further floor by floor on one side, the balconies allowing an intrusive view of those below. Laing's upstairs neighbor spots him sunbathing naked after nearly dropping a wine bottle on him. Those on the other side are cast in shadow under the floors above. It's uncomfortable either way. The apartments are nearly windowless, with horizontal slits above the eyeline, and walls are angled inward into oppressive triangles, the building closing in on its tenants. *High-Rise* director Ben Wheatley describes it as "a building that doesn't care about the people inside it."[14]

For all the architect's idealism, instead of a utopian communal experiment, the building becomes a microcosm of all the worst of the world beyond its parking lot. The distance from the high-rise to the rest of the city feels greater and greater as the tenants sink deeper into madness. London's city center may as well be in another state, another country, or beyond. Laing says, "Each day, the towers of central London seemed slightly more distant, the landscape of an abandoned planet receding slowly from his mind."[15]

It all starts to go wrong when the power goes out. Maintenance glitches become more frequent and last longer. When the resident documentarian, Richard Wilder (Luke Evans), rallies the kids at a birthday party, instigating a raid of the upper-floor adult swimming pool, it's an innocent revolutionary act of class rebellion. Until the electricity goes out permanently, triggering a rapid decline into a world of filth, violence, and debauchery. The supermarket is raided, and food supplies dwindle (alcohol remains in abundance). Fighting and sexual attacks are rampant. The all-important elevators are sabotaged, requiring militaristic maneuvers to get from floor to floor and trapping people inside. Garbage chutes are strategically clogged, creating barriers made of filth and rot. The failing electricity plunges the building into darkness once the sun goes down, encouraging illicit behavior, unbridled violence, and non-stop partying. Residents are reduced to primal survival mode, beloved pets become food, women trade sexual favors for safety, furniture becomes kindling, weapons are fashioned from golf clubs, and the once-coveted swimming pool is turned into a body pit, a fetid soup of rotting corpses. Leaving the building is an afterthought, a potential novelty, and moving is never considered. Laing is happier than he's ever been. In the book Ballard writes:

> *By its very efficiency, the high-rise took over the task of maintaining the social structure that supported them all. For the first time, it removed the need to repress every kind of anti-social behaviour and left them free to explore any deviant or wayward impulses. Secure within the shell of*

the high-rise…they were free to behave in any way they wished, explore the darkest corners they could find.

The goal of creating an idealized, safe environment fails at a rapid pace. Like most attempts at utopian self-sufficiency, the building does not live up to its expectations, and its inhabitants are incapable of living up to the challenge. The high-rise goes from luxurious efficiency to primitive chaos in a mere three months. The structure stands isolated in a barren area, the first completed and occupied building in a series of similar towers still under construction.

A prevailing ethos of modern architecture is its belief that design alone can shape people's lives and, by extension, the social life created around them. As Nathaniel Coleman writes: "A most valuable component of the absolutist utopianism that arguably characterized too much modern architecture was its earnest, albeit woefully naive, commitment to the betterment of society, supposedly achievable by making a new, better-organized, more hygienic, and often strangely parklike world over the traditional city."

In the film adaptation, the master builder of the high-rise — architect Anthony Royal (Jeremy Irons) — wonders how his experiment could have gone so wrong. "I conceived this building to be a crucible for change. I must have missed some vital element." The error may have been expecting that people would adapt to the buildings rather than adapting the buildings to suit the people.

In *High-Rise,* the elevator becomes the dividing line between the haves and the have-nots (or have-lesses). The elevators become the tools of power and control as the world inside becomes a nightmare of violence, garbage, human waste, and chaos. They are the border controls and the only means of survival. While apartment buildings, in one form or another, have existed since ancient Rome, the high-rise would not exist without the elevator. The higher we rise, the more important the ability to go down becomes. When the elevators stopped working at 20 Exchange Place in New York, the lives of those paying $5,000 a month for a one-bedroom apartment became a nightmare, stranding one tenant on the 43rd floor, while another woman with a broken foot was made to walk twenty-two flights to get to and from work. On the other end of the economic spectrum, the New York Housing Authority is notorious for its failure to fix broken elevators, leaving seniors and those with disabilities stranded in their homes. The broken elevator is a great equalizer.

Pruitt-Igoe resident Etta McCowan, April 1967, © Floyd Bowser/St Louis Post-Dispatch

The second, widely televised demolition of·a Pruitt-Igoe building that followed the March 16 demolition, U.S. Department of Housing and Urban Development, April 1972

In the famously failed Pruitt-Igoe public housing complex in St Louis, Missouri, the elevator system became a fundamental symptom of the building's neglect. They ran on a skip-stop system, stopping only at the fourth, seventh, and tenth floors, leaving tenants to walk up or down dark and dirty stairwells from one of the dismal gallery floor landings, "reminiscent of the caricatures of nineteenth-century insane asylums."[16] When they broke, tenants would be stuck in stalled cars reeking of urine, with no ventilation. Debris piled up in the elevator pits, and occasionally a tenant would step through the doors into a non-existent car, falling into the shaft.

Designed in 1954 by architect Minoru Yamasaki, (who would later create the also controversial and ill-fated World Trade Center in New York), Pruitt-Igoe replaced four hundred tenement buildings demolished in the name of "urban renewal." Consisting of thirty-three eleven-story buildings on the North side of St Louis, Pruitt-Igoe was conceived to create a new kind of planned community, one that would bring "'row house convenience' to high-rise dwellers."[17]

Like the fictional Starline Towers and the complex in *High-Rise*, Pruitt-Igoe also had a promotional film made extolling its conveniences and attributes. The narrator called it a "far cry from the crowded collapsing tenements that many of *these people* [emphasis mine] have known. Here in bright new buildings with spacious grounds, they can live…" There is an awkward dramatic pause after "live" as the camera pans over a group of Black girls in white dresses entering a school with brightly colored A, B, Cs on the windows. He continues, "…live with indoor plumbing, electric lights, fresh plastered walls and the rest of the conveniences that are expected in the twentieth century." In *The Pruitt-Igoe Myth* (2011), directed by Chad Freidrichs, former tenant Mrs Ruby Russell remembers that in the beginning "it was a very beautiful place, like a big hotel resort with plenty of green grass, trees, shrubbery, and all the works." When asked what happened, she replies, "Well, one day, we woke up, and it was all gone."

Doomed from the start, Pruitt-Igoe would become the prime example of how architecture is not the panacea for social ills that architects and city planners hoped it would be. Construction began in 1951, and before desegregation in 1955, the Pruitt side was designated for Black tenants and Igoe for white. After it became Pruitt-Igoe, white residents fled to the suburbs, and by 1958, of its nearly 10,000 official residents, 98 percent were Black with a median annual income of $2,300 (about $25,000 today). For those on public assistance, a stipulation for residence was that no able-bodied man could reside in the apartment, forcing families to split apart or fathers to hide their presence. "Pruitt-Igoe condenses into one 57-acre tract all of the problems and difficulties that arise from race and poverty, and all of the impotence, indifference, and hostility with which our society has so far dealt with these problems."[18] It became another slum, only bigger, taller, and vaster.

The amenities necessitated by its physical isolation were non-existent; as the crime rate rose, postal carriers stopped delivering packages, taxis refused to enter the grounds, and the police and fire department ignored calls. Without enough maintenance workers, garbage would pile up at the bottom of the elevator shafts, the stench wafting through the buildings. Broken windows would be boarded up instead of fixed, pipes leaked, and the heat would go out during sub-zero winters. Tenants were required to pay for basic repairs, but as vacancies increased, so did the costs. As the buildings emptied out, drug dealers moved in, and crime and fear became synonymous with Pruitt-Igoe. In 1967, a report conducted by the Pruitt-Igoe Neighborhood Corporation, entitled "A Dream Deferred," described the conditions:

> *A visitor driving or walking into Pruitt-Igoe is confronted with what looks like a disaster area. There are broken windows in every building. Streetlights are inoperative. Glass, rubble, tin cans, paper, and other debris litter the mud-caked walks. As the visitor nears a building entrance, the filth and debris intensify. The open rooms are receptacles for all manner of waste — mice, roaches, and other vermin thrive there. It takes little imagination to conceive of the dangers that lurk in these dark and filthy rooms. Incinerators, too small to accommodate the quantity of refuse placed in them, spill over; trash and garbage are heaped on the floors. Light bulbs and fixtures have disappeared; here and there, bare hot wires dangle from live sockets. The odor of decaying garbage is overpowering.*

This portrait of life in the building is strikingly similar to the state of the building in *High-Rise*, but unlike the people in Pruitt-Igoe, Laing and his fellow tenants rapidly (frighteningly rapidly) adapt to their new reality, accepting each worsening situation as it comes. The ease with which people in the high-rise slide into this vertical hell is unnerving, and telling in comparison to the residents of Pruitt-Igoe.

Rather than blame the project's ruination on the understaffed maintenance crews, the absence of any building management, or even on crime and vandalism (both arriving from poverty and systemic neglect), responsibility for the disaster fell on the tenants. The myth persisted that "people in low-income public housing do not know how to live." In truth, tenants complained and fought for years. After a particularly brutal winter, when the pipes burst, flooding the building with icy water, the tenants organized a rent strike, but to no avail.

Fifteen years after the first tenants moved in, conditions in the buildings were deemed too hazardous for occupation, and the whole thing was demolished in a spectacular explosion, images of which remain as the symbol of the failure of the public housing experiment. The video of the demolition of Pruitt-Igoe is mesmerizing. The massive cloud of smoke and debris blooms up from these huge structures slipping down into themselves, leaning into each other. It's known more for its destruction than for the people who lived there, and in reducing Pruitt-Igoe to a cautionary tale of urban planning, we risk forgetting the actual people whose lives these experiments were intended to improve. Some former tenants spoke fondly of their former home, holding on to the good despite the bad. In *The Pruitt-Igoe Myth*, one woman remembered a Christmas day when her neighbor turned the record player to face out the open door, blasted Martha and the Vandals, and everyone poured out of their apartments dancing:

> *I remember the Christmas lights, I remember the snow,*
> *I remember the rain, I remember the people, I remember*
> *people getting beat up, people having parties, I remember*
> *"Dancing in the Street." It was our home.*

Architecture as a virtuous pursuit has been a fundamental characteristic of modernism (if a slightly presumptuous one), "the belief that form not only could influence behavior but could actually shape it by transforming the individual and social life that came in contact with it." However, expecting people to rise to the challenge of architecture is rarely as successful a strategy as designing for people where they are.

The fallacy of Pruitt-Igoe was the presumption that bulldozing the old tenement buildings would erase the problems that came with them, that starting from scratch architecturally would mean starting from scratch socially. But the systemic economic and social inequality Pruitt-Igoe sought to solve didn't disappear, it just changed its veneer.

Instant Dystopias

"I went to the lift, but there was no need to press the electric knopka to see if it was working or not, because it had been tolchocked real horrorshow this night, the metal doors all buckled, some feat of rare strength indeed, so I had to walk the ten floors up. I cursed and panted climbing, being tired in plott if not so much in brain."

— *A Clockwork Orange,* Anthony Burgess

The utopian vision is always theoretical, and conceptual, perfect only to the little cut-out scale figures plopped into architectural renderings. Concrete would eventually swing from being the miracle material of the future to a symbol of urban decay. The first shot in Chris Cunningham's video for Aphex Twin's "Come to Daddy" (1997) looks up at a dingy, grey concrete apartment complex. The camera pans down, and we see an old woman walking her dog, a pile of garbage in a pool of stagnant water in the foreground. Out of the darkness of the building emerges a horde of children, each with the frozen, grinning face of frontman Richard D. James, little boys in hooded jackets, and girls in blue Peter-Pan-collared dresses with maniacal adult grins. The children run rampant, causing mayhem, led by a freakishly tall, ghoulish, naked creature of alien proportions who screams with gale-force wind into the face of the old woman. The six-minute horror movie was shot at the Thamesmead Council Estate, the same location where Stanley Kubrick filmed *A Clockwork Orange* in 1971, another movie about youth run amok.

After a night of ultra-violence and some milk-plus at the Korova Bar, Alex DeLarge (Malcolm McDowell) leaves his fellow Droogs and walks home through a garbage-strewn concrete complex to his home in Municipal Flat Block 18A, Linear North. Garbage has piled up in the corner of the lobby, the elevator is broken (of course), and on the wall is an expansive mural of near-naked male figures in the act of various types of work like a Greco-Roman WPA mural, the kind of public art intended to glorify the dignity of labor. Predictably there are dicks scrawled all over it.

A Clockwork Orange (1971) Collection Christophel © Warner Bros / Hawk films

Southmere estate, Thamesmead, London, UK / Cecilia Colussi Stock

There is an obvious correlation between the brutality of the architecture and the brutality of Alex and his Droogs. It's as if the dismal, flat, grey concrete, the hopelessness of the vandalized walls, and the trash-strewn hallways signify a nihilism that makes someone like Alex inevitable. But that correlation dissolves as soon as he walks through his parents' door. We're immediately hit by an explosion of colors, patterns, and textures: the entryway is papered in gold. In the living room each wall is a different color and texture: a deep blue with a whirly pattern; a pink wall and red ceiling; one wall is completely covered in shiny chrome domes. The bathroom wallpaper is a yellow-and-orange diamond pattern over silver, the same as in the dining area but with squares. His parents are doting and naive to the extent of their son's criminality, and the juxtaposing of their view of the world and their son's is made obvious in the deliriously maximalist décor.

Rather than building a set for an imagined place, Kubrick chose the newly built planned community of Thamesmead for the setting of his dystopian future. Only a few years old, it was simultaneously futuristic and already past its prime. Like similar planned communities, it never made it to the future it promised. McDowell described Thamesmead as "a vast, dismal, windswept collection of tower blocks connected by intimidating walkways. It was built as a social experiment, one of these places, sort of belabored and government-built, and of course, within ten years, it was a slum."[19]

Thamesmead was initially built in 1968 as an affordable solution to London's post-war housing shortage, a completely self-contained, poured-concrete town for the 21st century with houses, industries and offices, a shopping center, a clinic, schools, places of worship, and a marina. Despite the green spaces, walkways, and artificial lakes, it fell short of its promise. Lack of public transport cut it off from central London, and the shops and industries intended to serve the community and provide jobs never materialized. Built on marshland, houses were situated above street level to protect them from potential flooding. Roads and garages ran underneath, creating a network of concrete passages in the shadows. While the intentions might have been good, the streets became a no-man's-land where criminals and vandals could thrive unseen, leaving residents trapped on the level above. Financial mismanagement led to inadequate maintenance and its inevitable decline. For those in the city, "Thamesmead was just some weird town out in the middle of nowhere."[20]

The estate wasn't even finished when Kubrick chose it for his not-too-distant future. Did he see its potential for failure? Did he predict what it would become and just nudge it along in self-fulfilling prophecy? The problems facing Thamesmead would have existed whether he chose the location or not, but it certainly didn't help. The estate was only three years old when Alex smashed Georgie in the crotch with his walking stick, kicking him into the Flat Block Marina. It's a short time to go from an idyllic social experiment to an iconic symbol of urban blight and violence.

To combat the negative backlash from the film, the Greater London Council made *Living at Thamesmead* (1974), a short, fictionalized day-in-the-life movie extolling the estate's benefits. It opens with children riding bikes and splashing in the fountain and women pushing strollers past shops. A young couple takes a stroll arm-in-arm along the man-made lake (aka Flat Block Marina) to admire the abundant fish before stopping by the pub. Interestingly, there is a scene of a tenants' meeting in which they voice concerns about the lack of transportation as if to say, "Rest assured, we hear you." The film suggests that one could spend a whole day (every day) there and be entirely content. The conceit of Thamesmead or Pruitt-Igoe is that the architectural system of living they designed would be imbued in the lives of the residents. But you can't design people. The Ludovico Technique of behavioral conditioning worked about as well in urban planning as it did on Alex.

In the 2005 remake of the Japanese horror film *Dark Water*, Dahlia Williams (Jennifer Connelly) is in the middle of a custody battle with her ex-husband and needs to find an apartment for her and her five-year-old daughter, Cecilia (Ariel Gade). She's priced out of Manhattan and doesn't want to surrender and move closer to her ex-husband in Jersey City, so she picks a rather shoddy building for the cheap rent and proximity to a good school on Roosevelt Island, a small piece of land on the East River.

As the real estate agent shows her around, he reassures her that the super will mop up the rain puddle in the elevator and that the lobby is due for a new paint job that will really brighten the place up. Walking the dingy hallway to the apartment, he gives her a bit of history on the place. "The building is built in the Brutalist style. What they were trying to create was a little village. A utopia really is what they had in mind." Director Walter Salles chose the Eastwood Apartments for the location, and it is indeed what they had in mind. Designed by Corbusier protégé Josep Lluis Sert in 1969, the apartment complex/village was part of a masterplan to create a new community on "the Island Nobody Knows," a little city next to the City.

The Island Nobody Knows, 1969, Philip Johnson and John Burgee, © The Metropolitan Museum of Art

The Landing (Eastman Apartments), author photo

Like in *High-Rise*, *Shivers*, and Thamesmead, the film's location is isolated from the "mainland." It's both "the City" and not. On the tramway (a quaint but antiquated way to cross the river), headed to their new neighborhood, Cecilia complains that they aren't in the city. Her mother tells her it's just a different part of the city. Cecilia shakes her head and says, "That's not the city. *That's* the city," pointing back to Manhattan. An elderly man looks over his newspaper and says, "She's right." In most horror movies, a car pulls up to a big, beautiful house, the kids spill out, running to their new home with excitement. When Dahlia and her daughter first enter the building, the entryway is dismal, run-down, and dimly lit a sickly green. Cecilia notes, "This is yucky. This place is yucky." Cecilia tells it like it is.

In the nineteenth century, Roosevelt Island, then known as Blackwell's Island (nicknamed "Farewell Island"), was the place where New York City sent its undesirables. It was home to a penitentiary, a workhouse, a smallpox hospital (whose ruins remain there), and the New York City Lunatic Asylum, where in 1887, journalist Nellie Bly had herself committed to expose the inhumane conditions. Blackwell's was renamed Welfare Island in 1921, and continued to be used as an enclave for the imprisoned and the chronically ill. By the 1960s, "Manhattan's unloved stepchild" was all but abandoned and looked upon with an "unease and distaste that has its roots in centuries of scandal and horror." What was to be done with this "ghostly relic of a grim, malodorous past."[21]

In 1968, Mayor John V. Lindsay put out a call for proposals for a mixed-use master plan. One submission was a *Poltergeist*-esque concept that involved digging up the bodies in Queens and Brooklyn cemeteries and reburying them on the Island to free up space in the two Boroughs. That's a movie I'd like to see. The chosen master plan developed by Philip Johnson and John Burgee included housing for 20,000 people, primarily for a middle-to low-income community, with "a larger proportion of multibedroom apartments in this Island Town than is usual in New York City: the reason is to make families with children more at home."[22]

The Town, as Johnson and Burgee called it, has only one street devoted to vehicles, and an elaborate underground pneumatic tube system attached to all the buildings for garbage collection (this still exists). Along Main Street are restaurants, shops, and a library, with signage unified in red Helvetica. It's an image of what they thought the future would look like in 1969, but one that was impossible to maintain for a future that would never come.

The irony of the estate agent referring to this outmoded building as a utopian experiment is lost on Dahlia as she surveys the space with sad resignation: the windows don't open; the "two-bedroom" is really a large one-bedroom. The compact kitchen table, folded up for maximum efficiency, which may have seemed a clever use of space when it was new, looks old and sad now. Utopias shouldn't require a sales pitch.

A reoccurring theme in my nightmares concerns leaks in ceilings: black holes opening above me and water pouring down into my clean dry home, ruining all my things. A few years ago, I had a leak in my bathroom ceiling. Water would pool into my light fixture, filling up like a bowl. Damp blisters formed above me, the paint stretching like skin, pimples waiting to burst at any minute. I would brush my teeth with one eye trained on the ceiling. I complained and complained to the management and the superintendent that this was going to blow any minute now. And it did. I woke one night to a horrible crash as the ceiling came down, leaving a two-foot diameter gaping wound above me and a bathroom covered in wet drywall. It was an ugly, messy opening that made me feel vulnerable and exposed. There was a *hole* where there shouldn't be a hole, and that is never good. Nothing evokes more dread to me than the phrase "I'll patch it up in a couple of days when it's dry."

On the first day in their new apartment, a wet, black stain begins to show through the ceiling of Cecilia's room. It gets larger and larger each day, becoming more grotesque, less like water damage and more like disease dripping brackish water on to her bed. They assume at first that it's those "darn teenagers" breaking into the apartment and turning on all the taps just to be assholes, but the real problem is far worse and much harder to fix. A little girl, abandoned by her parents, accidently drowned in the water tower, and the result is the spirit of a very angry child in need of a mother. As the film progresses, the stain gets bigger, spreads wider. This is a trope we see all the time: an ominous crack in the wall revealing something hidden in the crawl space, scuff marks on floorboards where furniture that shouldn't be moved was moved, a bit of peeling wallpaper revealing something underneath, common enough anomalies that can easily be shrugged off as normal wear and tear. The rapid growth of the stain and its spread could be mold but is clearly not. The dilapidation is a signal from a dead girl trying to make herself known.

In *High-Rise*, the physical decline of the building (broken elevator, power outages, and the build-up of garbage) is indicative of a horrific, mass descent into madness. In *Dark Water* the deterioration is a given — the leaks are inevitable, it's something to be expected, and the poltergeist activity is hidden in plain sight. Poor maintenance becomes complicit in the haunt. The superintendent who refuses to fix the plumbing is the same super who failed to notice the little girl left alone in the apartment upstairs. The door to the roof is left open when it should be closed, giving the girl access to the water tower. The old washing machine where Dahlia sees a little girl spinning in the dirty soapy water is in a dark and isolated laundry room where she is confronted by a young man threatening to attack her. The noises above her head are assumed to be vandals and junkies squatting in the apartment above. As opposed to the overtly bizarre and unexplainable phenomenon of most haunted houses, the disturbances Dahlia experiences feel dismal but ordinary. While the giant, gaping hole in the ceiling might evoke abject horror, it's not an uncanny experience. It's an old building with bad plumbing and it's the only thing she can afford.

In 2005, the Ennis House, after years of neglect, rain, and earthquakes, was listed by the National Trust for Historic Preservation as one of America's most endangered places. For all its good intentions, concrete is not the panacea it was thought to be. While it may seem indestructible and eternal, concrete does not age as well as one might think. Its decay is invisible. Moisture seeps into the porous material, rusting the rebar used for reinforcement, causing it to deteriorate from the inside out. The clean, crisp grey gets dingy and stained over time, and the monumental apartment complexes that have outlived their innovative intention are left to neglect. Aging brutalist buildings have a particular melancholy about them, a testament to failed idealism. Whether it's a public complex to house thousands or a modernist compound for a single billionaire, time comes for concrete equally.

There is a mistrust of domestic modernism, architecture made for Bond villains, criminal ring lords, and billionaires, not families. There is a persistent belief that concrete equals cold, and design takes precedence over people. Minimalism suggests a luxury of space, with expansive blank walls meant to display collections of monumental art on properties isolated enough to preclude the fear of neighbors peeking through walls of glass. Clutter is anathema to a manicured life.

When Kanye West and his then wife Kim Kardashian commissioned designer Axel Vervoordt to transform a $60-million McMansion in Calabasas, California, into a "futuristic Belgian monastery," they "changed the house by purifying it, and we kept pushing to make it purer and purer." [23] That purity is uncompromisingly literal, with minimal furnishing, bare walls, and a neutral palette of various shades of white. But in 2021, the now divorced Ye purchased a $57-million oceanfront house in Malibu designed by famed Pritzker Prize–winning Japanese architect Tadao Ando, and then paid contractor Tony Saxon to destroy it. For his vision of a "bomb shelter from the 1910s," [24] the expansive floor-to-ceiling sea green glass windows of the ocean-facing façade were all broken, leaving the house exposed to the elements. At his request, doors were removed, electrical power, heating, and plumbing were dismantled, and bathroom fixtures and kitchen appliances were taken out, negating any semblance of human presence and reducing it to a crumbling shell with rusted railings resembling the remnants of a war that hasn't happened yet. With pristine houses on either side, the house is a designed ruin from a very isolated and singular post-apocalyptic disaster, a modernist folly.

Owen Hatherly writes that the imperative of the Modernist was to build a new world in the ruins of the old: "But what of it if the new society never emerged? We have been cheated out of the future, yet the future's ruins lie about us hidden or ostentatiously rotting." [25] As Dr. Robert Laing muses while spit-roasting a dog's leg on the balcony of his high-rise apartment, "Sometimes he found it difficult not to believe they were living in a future that had already taken place." Whatever Ye's motives for speeding up the aging process on his status symbol home (the result of a manic episode on the part of a megalomaniacal billionaire, or petty revenge against his ex-wife, who always wanted an Ando), he inadvertently created the modernist future we dread: homes decimated to the point of dismal debris, without protection or comfort; a house of bare, diseased bones where our ideal visions of a new way of living are abandoned to rot and rust. Unlike Wright's hope, it is neither permanent, noble, nor beautiful. The future never had a chance.

Witch Houses

Your Friendly Neighborhood Hag

"There was this old house in the neighborhood where I grew up. The old lady who lived there had like a hundred cats. So everyone called her Old Hag, Witch Lady. Every Halloween, all the kids would egg her house. Same house, different town."

— *House of the Witch* (2017)

The outside of the house of my dreams would look like no one lives there: overgrown ivy crawls up the side of the walls; the lawn is a bit wild, it could use a fresh coat of paint. My dream house would be the opposite of inviting. It would be the house with the creepy lady and all the cats, the one that inspires local urban legends, the doorbell kids dare each other to ring on Halloween. Then one day, some brave kid will knock on my door, I'll greet them politely, maybe offer a lemonade, give them some money to mow the lawn, and they'll realize the creepy old lady is actually pretty cool. Perhaps my affinity for decay is due to my having grown up in Detroit in the '80s, so decrepit Victorian mansions were part of my natural landscape. Perhaps it's also that I prefer, for the most part, to be left alone. When I described my fantasy house to a friend she said, "So you want to inspire fear?" "Yes!" I replied.

There is a characteristic associated with the "witch house" that has little to do with whoever may live there: the house is usually old, in disrepair, unmaintained or uncared for, and seemingly abandoned (whether it actually is or not). It is probably quiet and dark most of the time. There's no sign of children, and it's therefore not welcoming to children. There's probably at least one cat. It is a house that does not participate in the social world around it: there are no Christmas lights hanging off the roof, no backyard barbecues or basketball hoops in the driveway. People know a witch house when they see it, even if they never see who's inside. If the house was a woman (as most houses are), its human proxy would be compatible, a certain type of woman we have been taught to fear, pity, and avoid becoming at all cost: post-menopausal, living alone, and abandoned by society long ago; the "crazy cat lady"; the Miss Havishams, the Norma Desmonds, the Blanche and "Baby" Jane Hudsons.

There is a correlation between the state of the house, its age and decrepitude, and the woman who inhabits it. The home is synonymous with family and domesticity, and the house has long been considered the intrinsic domain of women. Houses and the women who inhabit them have a complicated relationship, the nature of one informing that of the other. The quality of one being judged against the other. There is something wrong with the house, so there must be something wrong with the woman. The house is monstrous, so the woman who lives there must be a monster.

I want to clarify what I mean when I talk about "witches." First there is our collective cultural understanding of mythical witches of folk tales, storybooks, horror movies, and Halloween costumes. Then there are real witches: practitioners of magick and hoodoo, brujas, Wiccans, and neo-pagans. But then there is a more all-encompassing definition, which I use as my guide; what Pam Grossman refers to as a "figure of transgressive female power." [1] Carmen Maria Machado clarifies:

> *She is a woman, single, and childless. She has her own little house, which she may or may not share with an animal. She is an artist, or a craftswoman, or a scientist, if you imagine magic as a kind of science. She is wily, self-satisfied, and in charge of her own affairs. She commands respect… She is what happens when women get to direct the warp and weft of their own lives.* [2]

The prosecution of aberrant women has a long history. In Europe, of the 80,000 people put to death for witchcraft in the fifteenth through the seventeenth centuries, the vast majority were widowed women over the age of fifty who lived alone. Even if you were married, you could be accused of witchcraft for not having enough children. During the Salem Witch Trials of 1692, the majority of the women accused were marginalized women on the fringes of society. They were poor single mothers and wealthy independent widows. In the case of Tituba, an enslaved Indigenous woman, her powerlessness made her an easy scapegoat. They were either problematic women whose lives challenged Puritan patriarchal norms, or they were simply just not liked.

What a witch looks like has changed over the decades from the toxic-green Wicked Witch of the West or her bubbly counterpart Glenda. There's the statuesque glamor of the Evil Queen or her old-hag alter ego in *Snow White & the Seven Dwarves*. There are the normcore witches and their hippie aunts of *Practical Magic*, or the goth girls of *The Craft*. The places where the witch lives are just as varied: The Evil Queen lived in an appropriately intimidating gothic castle perched high on top of a mountain. The quirky Owen sisters of *Practical Magic* lived in a large, Second Empire house in a quaint New England town. In *Bewitched*, Tabitha Stevens lived in a modest Tudor-style house in the suburbs. The seventeenth-century domain of Robert Eggers' *The Witch* is a crude, rudimentary structure of sticks and leaves, suggesting something ancient and from nature.

The homes of adult women who are not married, not straight, not AFAB (assigned female at birth), who do not have children or ever intend to have them are transgressions like the women themselves. *Häxan*, the Swedish silent film made in 1922, is a kind of illustrated lecture about the history of witchcraft, and is our first depiction of a witch on film. It's the year 1488, and we're introduced to the witch in her home. She is a small, cloaked old woman stirring some mysterious concoction brewing in a cauldron over a fire. Suspended from the ceiling is the skeleton of a small animal, and in the corner, on the shelf above a couple of barrels, is a human skull. Two companions, both old women, one with a hunchback, come by bringing a delivery of bundles of sticks, one containing the severed hand of a thief stolen from the gallows. The other takes a seat and helps herself to a drink before taking some frogs and snakes from a bag and putting them in a pot. A visitor comes knocking on their basement door, a woman hoping to get a love potion. It's a day in the life of a witch, and it is all rather cozy and homey. Despite her dipping a severed finger in a barrel to soak like a tea bag, the witch's home is essentially a common domestic space, a *Golden Girl* household, albeit with less pastel, of old women sitting around the cauldron eating cheesecake. Or eye of newt.

Häxan, 1922

Aside from simply being a residence where a witch happens to live, a witch house may serve a dual purpose: either to scare or entice. It may drive people away with its decay or grim atmosphere, or lure people in with its comfort or opulence. While the style or intent might vary, the witch house eschews domesticity as the central purpose of the home and the matriarch as a caretaker. Instead, it frames the house as a locus of power. The witch's house, the place where aberrant women live, has become a symbol of both enchantment and dread. What defines the home is often what defines the woman, and the witch's house serves a different purpose. It serves the witch and her needs only.

Magical Trap Houses

If you were to close your eyes and picture a witch, I would bet the image of a woman in a black cloak with a black pointed hat holding a broom would be the first thing to come to mind. In her exhibition *Major Arcana: Witches in America*, photographer Frances F. Denny shows us contemporary practicing witches at home all over the country: New Orleans, Maine, Los Angeles, Salem, Vermont, Brooklyn (so many from Brooklyn). The women are as varied and unique as any other cross section of a culture, but they each exude a quality of self-assured confidence and the comfort that comes with being at home in their bodies and at home in their space. Some give off strong witchy energy, with long black robes, an abundance of accessories, and Stevie Nicks shawls, but one woman is in surgical scrubs as if she just came off a shift. Others are in simple flowered sun dresses like they came straight from the farmers' market. Some are in hippie tie-dye, others in black Eileen Fisher basics. None of them look boring.[3]

If I asked you to describe her house (the witch with the pointy hat and the broom), it would probably be a small cottage, made of wood or stone, with a peaked roof and perhaps a vaguely "old world" look. My guess is you didn't picture a tract house in a subdivision. There is a precedent for this image of the small cottage. In Slavic folklore, Baba Yaga is an enigmatic character with a penchant for eating children. She is described as a grotesque old woman whose home is a small hut supported by two giant chicken legs, surrounded by a fence mounted with skulls. The door to her hut faces the forest, and when she comes home, riding in her giant mortar, Baba Yaga commands her house to turn around so she may enter.

Spadena House, Kafziel, 2011

Baba Yaga's Hut, Ivan Bilibin, 1899

But it was Hollywood that solidified the iconic witch-house style. In 1921, art director Harry Oliver built the Spadena House (known as the Witch House) for offices and dressing rooms for the Irvin Willat movie studio. Inspired by the illustrations in old fairy tale books, he created a caricature of a medieval cottage with exaggerated pointed and lopsided roofs, warped shingles, loose window shutters, and irregularly curved walls and door frames. It looks like a cartoon interpretation of a three-hundred-year-old European country cottage on the verge of collapse. In 1926 it was moved to Beverly Hills and turned into a private home, sparking a trend of storybook architecture. Houses sprang up all over Los Angeles as if plucked from a Disney movie. The Spadena House is more whimsical than frightening, an imagineered amusement turned residential house. While it may look quaint, quirky, and trick-or-treater friendly, it has none of the magic allure or foreboding energy I imagine a witch house to have. Unlike a particularly strange dance school in Berlin.

Mother's House

"Me, Varelli, an architect living in London, met the Three Mothers and designed and built for them three dwelling places. One in Rome, one in New York, and the third in Freiburg, Germany. I failed to discover until too late that from those three locations the Three Mothers rule the world with sorrow, tears, and darkness."

— *Inferno* (1980)

Dario Argento's *Inferno*, the thematic sequel to *Suspiria* (1977), begins with a woman reading from *The Three Mothers*, a book/confession by architect and alchemist E. Varelli. The book begins with an admission: "I built these horrible houses. The repositories for all their filthy secrets." He adds that these "mothers" are actually "evil stepmothers, incapable of giving life," continuing a tradition of blaming, if not motherhood per se, then a non-biological 'replacement' mother". Even the building's foundations are evil. "The land upon which the three houses have been constructed will eventually become deathly and plague-ridden, so much so that the area all around will reek horribly."

Varelli built these houses to be the "eyes and ears" of the Mothers, acting as proxies for the witches, like architectural familiars, and Rose Elliot suspects her apartment building in New York may be one of these "horrible residences." But aside from a tell-tale sickly stench, a corpse submerged in a flooded basement, and holes in the walls for whispering secrets from apartment to apartment, Mother Tenebrarum's house is rather passive compared to its sister in Germany. Varelli seems to have used up most of his creativity for Mother Suspiriorum's place.

Suspiria, Dario Argento (1977) / Prod DB Â© Seda Spettacoli /DR / Alamy
Stock Photo

In *Suspiria*, American ballet student Suzy Bannion (Jessica Harper) comes to Freiburg, Germany, to attend a prestigious dance academy. Unbeknownst to her, it happens to be run by a coven of witches. The Tanz Dance Academy building is bright salmon pink with gold details, providing just a hint of whimsey and color that feels suspiciously conspicuous. Argento used a real location for the exterior, a late Gothic bourgeois house built in 1516 called Haus zum Walfisch (Whale House), likely as a reference to the story of Jonah. Just like the Biblical fisherman, Suzy is swallowed up by the house, trapped in the belly of the beast, albeit a much more outrageously ostentatious and luxurious one. When Suzy walks through the door, she is engulfed in velvety blue walls, oversized pointed arches framed in glistening black, and a stairwell with a serpentine gold railing. The hallway to the students' living quarters is papered in red velvet brocade. The key to the witches' secret room is hidden in the floral murals of the pale green administrator's office, and the hallway to their chamber is deep yellow and ochre with mysterious text in gold.

The lobby of the students' apartment building is a field of pink, blue, and red in sharp geometric shapes, a Technicolor *Cabinet of Dr. Caligari*. The symmetry and relentlessness of pattern and color is disorienting in its artifice. The bedroom wallpapers are a bold pattern of black and white flowers on one wall, and on the other is a pink, white, and grey interpretation of Escher's *Sky and Water I,* a signal that this space, this world, is illusory. The exterior, the lobby of the school, the student's apartment: every location feels like a visual conjuration. Vincenzo Natali says, "Argento presents us with a series of escalating set pieces so that the film winds itself up like a spinning ballerina into a state of hysteria."[4]

Scenes are filtered with red and blue lighting, giving it the tinge of a Technicolor fairy tale. Argento was purposefully "trying to reproduce the color of Walt Disney's *Snow White*," going so far as to use the same film stock as they did in the 1950s.[5] There are no black cloaks or grey stone walls at the Tanz Academy. The primary color palette is surreal, jarring, and completely destabilizing from the way we are used to seeing horror. It's decadent, luxurious, dramatic, and distinctly feminine.

There is one moment that emphasizes the difference between the interior magical space and the world outside the academy. One of the students has gone missing and Suzy goes to see her psychiatrist (played by Udo Kier) in the hope he can shed some light on her disappearance. They meet outside of a convention center and we are suddenly back in a world of natural lighting, poured concrete planters, and rational explanations for bizarre behavior. The space of diagnostics and reason is oppressively beige.

The dance academy is the public front covering the real purpose of the building: it is the home and headquarters of a coven, a place of matriarchal power. There is an ostentatious confidence to the Tanz Academy décor. It features neither black cloaks in the dark of night nor soft and gentle pastels, but pure saturation of power through color. Its vibrancy is aggressive and intimidating. It is not a safe space for the uninitiated, and those who try to undermine their work could find themselves in a glowing bright blue pit of razor wire. While the space is far from gloomy, it's also not inviting, soothing, or comforting. Unlike a cozy little cottage in the woods made of candy.

Holda's House

"I assumed a disguise of old age to make myself seem kind and weak. I built for us a house, one with a proper kitchen and a dining room."

— *Gretel & Hansel* (2020)

In Nobuhiko Ôbayashi's horror/comedy/psychedelic fever dream *Hausu* (1977), Gorgeous (Kimiko Ikegami) invites her school friends[6] to spend their summer break with her at her aunt's house in the countryside. When they arrive, the house looms over the girls as a hand-painted two-dimensional backdrop rising high into a bright blue sky. A stone wall encompassed in tall grass and flowered creeping vines frames the entry with fairy-tale charm, the conspicuous artifice designating the entry into a magical space. As the doors part, Auntie (Yōko Minamida) is revealed sitting primly in a wheelchair with a fluffy white cat on her lap, a perfect silver bob haircut, large sunglasses, and a deceptive, welcoming smile.

Inside the house is dark and dusty, dripping with cobwebs and neglect. Auntie feigns helplessness, a feeble old woman unable to tend to her house properly, and the girls enthusiastically offer to take up the cooking and cleaning. But as the girls make themselves at home, they begin to disappear one by one, and Auntie, no longer in a wheelchair, is getting stronger and stronger. Turns out Auntie died long ago waiting for her fiancé, killed in WWII, to come home to her. Now her ghost is entwined with the house and eats any unmarried girls who cross its threshold. While Auntie dances with a skeleton and helps herself to a snack of a human arm, Mac's decapitated head replaces a watermelon cooling in the well, a ceiling lamp grabs Kung Fu by the head, whipping her around the room, the piano swallows up Melody and bites off her fingers, and finally, Gorgeous herself becomes possessed by the house, taking the place of her aunt.

The girls in *Hausu* fell victim to a common assumption about older women: that Auntie would have an innate nurturing nature and a grandmotherly instinct to care for children, all children. It's one of my all-time favorite witch ruses: feign frailty, lure them in with the promise of safety and a warm meal, then, when they least expect it, have them for dinner. Auntie did it, Baba Yaga did it, and the witch with a house made of baked goods did it.

As the 1812 Brothers Grimm story goes, Hansel and Gretel's parents are too poor to feed them all, so their mother, with little opposition from their father, kicks them out into the forest to fend for themselves (as one did in medieval Europe). Thinking he's smart, Hansel leaves a trail of pebbles and breadcrumbs along the way, hoping it will guide them home. It doesn't work. On the third day of wandering the woods and slowly starving to death, "they came to a little house made of bread with cake for a roof and pure sugar for windows." Hansel helps himself to a bit of the roof, while Gretel finishes off a few small windows, when they hear a shrill voice coming from the house: "Nibble, nibble, I hear a louse! Who's that nibbling on my house?"

Hansel and Gretel in front of the witch's house, Otto Kubel, 1930

The owner of the shrill voice invites them in, serves them pancakes and apples, and gives them warm beds to sleep in, all the while plotting to kill, cook, and eat them. They wake up the next morning with Hansel locked in a chicken coop, and in a particularly cruel twist, the witch commands Gretel to cook food for her brother to fatten him up and to fetch the water to boil him. After a month (a month!) of this, the witch has had enough, and decides she is going to eat this kid whether he's fat enough or not. She tells Gretel to get in the oven and check on the bread she's baking, a scheme to push her in and cook her too, but Gretel performs a genius act of weaponized incompetence. She pretends she doesn't know how to do it and asks the witch to show her. When she does, Gretel pushes her in, bolts the oven door, and the siblings make their escape leaving the witch to burn to death. They steal her jewels and take them home to their now wealthy, loving father. It ends simply: "However, the mother had died."

As in the Grimms' story, in Osgood Perkins' *Gretel & Hansel* (2020), Gretel (Sophia Lillis) and Hansel (Sam Leakey) are kicked out of their impoverished home and abandoned in the forest to make it on their own or die trying. Along with the hierarchical reversal of the names and the larger age distinction between them (Gretel is sixteen and Hansel is eight), the most obvious divergence from the original is that the witch house isn't made of food. While the image of a house made of gingerbread and candy is an alluring temptation to a child, this is not a child's story, but one about a young woman "standing on the threshold of her own experience." And this time it's the father who dies.

Gretel's mother sends her to the home of a wealthy man in the hopes of becoming a housekeeper, but when during their introduction he asks if she's still a virgin, she declines the job. When Gretel rebukes her mother's directive to go to the convent, she tells her daughter, "Then the two of you can start work digging your sweet little graves. When you and your brother take up your little shovels, dig a hole for mommy too." When they leave, there is no trail of pebbles or breadcrumbs to lead them back home. There is no going back.

With no prospects or food, they wander the forest, accidentally getting high off some shrooms, until, like all witch stories, they come across a house in the forest just when they need it. Hansel gleefully exclaims that it smells of cake (and bacon). Gretel notes that there's a slide with no signs of any children.

Gretel and Hansel (2020), directed by Oz Perkins

The directive given to production designer Jeremy Reed was that the house couldn't look like anything we've seen before. It couldn't be the cutesy candy-cane-trimmed gingerbread house or the classic, rustic Arthur Rackham illustrations. It's not like there haven't been new takes on the classic candy house. In *Hansel & Gretel: Witch Hunters* (2013) the house is sickeningly sweet, almost grotesque, and is far creepier than its predecessors. The roof is entirely coated with a thick, viscous icing. The circular door is trimmed with glistening rainbow candy around a ring of whitish candy corn set in gooey pink resembling a cross between a mouth and an anus. But it's still an edible house.

Jeremy Reed's house is both ominous and alluring. The only color is the orange glow emanating from the windows, which is both eerie and inviting. Perkins admits the curving art-nouveau window frames came straight from the windows in *Suspiria*. From outside, Gretel looks through a peephole in the door and sees a long table brimming with food. From the inside her eye is framed by a triangle, forming an Eye of Providence.

Reed's design is matte black on black, minimal, and slightly

Nordic, and sits like a witch hat in a forest clearing with a long rectangular wing to the right side. It is, as Reed says, a "Stealth Bomber"[7] of a house. It's a combination of an A-frame structure with mid-century, flat-top, post-and-beam architecture, with Quaker and Mennonite influences. Reed also looked at malevolent architecture, like Albert Speer's severe and monumental constructions, which explains the somewhat questionable choice of the pattern of six-pointed stars on the door. Considering the inflammatory history of blood libel accusations and the Grimm Brothers' anti-Semitism, the intent behind this detail isn't entirely clear. In an interview, Reed explained that the chevron was in reference to the gates of Auschwitz, a signal that through the door there is only death, but I'm not sure if that meaning comes through. It's just a short moment, a small detail of black on black, but obvious enough to question.

Enter Holda (Alice Krige). She ducks down slightly as she emerges from the house; the doors are just a bit smaller than they should be: child sized. Like her house, the witch is severe, but charming, with just a hint of ulterior motive. Holda's silhouette forms a triangle (a visual theme that will repeat throughout the film). Her pointed hat and the square shoulders of the cloak fall in a long A-shape to the ground. Her form is geometric, an extension of her house. She invites the children to her table, which is perpetually and inconceivably bursting with hot cooked meats, bread, cakes, and fresh fruits, despite there being no obvious source for the food. The plums are ripe despite being out of season; the unsalted ham never rots; there's always fresh milk, but there's no cow in sight. It is a ridiculously overabundant meal for one woman alone. Gretel assumes that, with all the food, there must be guests on the way. "Guests?" Holda answers. "I'd rather have roaches." Gretel makes the mistake of referring to her as "Mrs." Holda answers, "You think I'm married? To a ball and chain at my heel?" When Holda asks what they were doing in her woods "so charmingly unchaperoned," Gretel explains that their mother has come upon hardship. Holda responds, "Usually the first thing a mother comes upon."

Holda takes a special interest in Gretel. In the original tale, the witch mainly uses Gretel as a housekeeper, but in this case Holda sees her potential, encouraging her to access her own powers, to embrace her independence and rid herself of the burden of her little brother. She is a decidedly non-maternal yet nurturing figure. Nurturing to Gretel at least. Holda reminds Gretel, she's not the boy's mother. Hansel reminds Gretel that Holda is not their mother. Out of frustration with Hansel and his growing suspicion of his sister's attachment to this stranger, Gretel kicks him out into the forest (as their mother did). Regretting her cruelty the next morning, she is dismayed to find him still gone. Looking for him, she discovers a small door in the back of a closet opening upon an impossibly long stairway, far deeper than seems plausible. It leads to an immense open space with a twenty-four-foot-high ceiling and white brick walls, with the bottom few feet stained a rusty red from blood. Unlike the warm homey wood of the upstairs, the downstairs is cold and utilitarian. Like a morgue. Going down into the basement is a transitional experience, the stairs a gateway between the domestic space of the home and the magical space where the sausage gets made, literally. In the middle of the room is a long table piled with bloody limbs and organs, the dismembered remains of children. Holda, now young, with a patchwork of sigil tattoos down her arms, waves her black-stained fingers and the grotesque assortment of human flesh and guts turns into a feast of cooked meats, cheeses, bread, and fruits.

The house has multiple levels of malevolence. Outside, the ominous jet-black house is a suspiciously convenient refuge.

Inside is a homey, domestic space with an absurd amount of food, where Holda teaches Gretel how to nurture her burgeoning magical power. Deeper still, the interior of the interior is the basement, the real kitchen, where the children are led to their deaths. The witch house in both *Hansel & Gretel* and *Gretel & Hansel* functions as a Trojan horse/house where the inside and the outside do not match.[8] The exterior is knowable, identifiable, and while extraordinary (either made of candy or architecturally exceptional), it is still recognizable as a house and therefore safe. Specifically, it is the home of "a small, ancient woman," as the Grimms say. In *Gretel & Hansel* it is not just the house but Holda herself that offers food, comfort, and compassion. She disarms with age and frailty, manipulating our assumption that to be old and female is to be congenitally nurturing and physically helpless. In *Hansel & Gretel* the house is designed to be tempting to children to an absurd degree. In *Gretel & Hansel*, the house doesn't have to be constructed out of candy and gingerbread, it only needs to be there just when they need it the most.

Boro's House

"Imagine he's a house and you're wandering around. Imagine that you're inside him. Now break something."
— *Brand New Cherry Flavor* (2021)

Architecture is often described as a mediator between the body and the environment. In Nick Antosca's *Brand New Cherry Flavor*, architecture is a mediator between minds as well. Fresh from film school, Lisa Nova (Rosa Salazar) moves to Los Angeles, determined to make and (most importantly) direct her first movie. Producer Lou Burke (Eric Lange) offers to take her under his wing, options the movie, and promises to introduce her to the right people to get her movie made, promises that he will inevitably break.

On the way to a party to meet some Very Important People, he does what the central-casting "sleazy Hollywood producer" does when a young, hopeful woman whose career he holds in his hands is in the passenger seat of his car. He puts his hand on her upper thigh and says, "I think we make a good team." Lisa firmly removes his hand from her leg and says, "I think we make a good team too." At the party he heads to the men's room, and she's left disillusioned, shaken, and very, very angry. Meanwhile, there's an older woman in the crowd with a mane of wavy auburn hair that falls into the wide fur collar around her neck, blending with the cat she snuggles to her powdered cheek, and she's been staring Lisa down since she arrived.

She introduces herself as Boro (Catherine Keener), as if Lisa should have known that already. She exudes the calm, self-assuredness of someone who knows they are the most powerful person in the room. She tells Lisa, "That man you came with? He's having a very important conversation without you." Like Holda, Boro appears just when she's needed and guides Lisa through a telepathic thought experiment. It's an elegant kind of a spell, envisioning the self as a house one can enter at will and wreak havoc. What Lisa pictures in her mind's eye is a secret to us; we don't know how she's envisioned being inside Burke, or what she's chosen to break, but it works. Burke returns from the men's room with a deal excluding Lisa from her own movie and also a nosebleed. Boro offers Lisa her unique services to "hurt someone" for her, and like Holda, she offers her power and dominion over all things. Or at least over Lou Burke. Lisa just has to throw up a kitten now and then as payment. (That's not a metaphor.)

Boro's home looks abandoned. It's a white Greek Revival

mansion with two-story columns and massive windows that look like they haven't been opened in decades. It is large and opulent, but seems ignored. Overgrown trees and plants crawl up the sides of the building, there's weatherworn furniture on the porch, and the front door is covered in graffiti. Like Holda's house, Boro's house has a public-facing façade and a magical space in the interior. Entering Boro's world means bypassing what one would assume was the main entrance to the house. When enemies come to visit, she invites them in through the front door. When Lisa arrives, she walks through a side entryway marked with a mural of a white jaguar and steps into a veritable rainforest. Working her way through this indoor jungle, brushing away massive tropical leaves, it's not clear if they are inside or outside or both at the same time. Boro sits in a clearing where she mixes her potions, does some tattooing, and details custom leather jackets for her personal crew of zombie minions. The tile floor and greenhouse window panes in the background give little hints that they are inside of something, but where or when isn't as clear. It could be Los Angeles in the 1990s, or a South American jungle hundreds of years ago.

After the curse against Burke is cast, Lisa goes home with a parting gift from Boro, a small potted plant. Lisa's apartment isn't abandoned, but she is (inexplicably) the only tenant in the building. It's a bit worn, the pink walls could use freshening, and the furnishings are remnants from years of previous tenants. The aura of the bygone days of Hollywood lingers in the air.[9]

She wakes up the next day to find the little plant has grown up the wall and down through the floor into the apartment below. Boro's jungle is materializing in Lisa's apartment, and the invasive species that is Boro has spread throughout her home, turning her safe space into a magical one. In her bedroom, a trapdoor has materialized in the floor, leading down, not to the apartment below, but to a vast dark space, empty except for the ladder leading her down and a chaise lounge sofa upholstered in jaguar fur. The sofa may be Lisa's long-lost mother or the spirit of Boro's lover (an actual jaguar) from about nine hundred years ago when she/he was a Columbian shaman. The porous nature of the connection between Boro and Lisa is both psychological and physical, and it's manifested through their homes.

But Boro is a home invader in more ways than one. S/He has the ability to hop into a body of his choosing and take residence, suppressing their consciousness and taking control. The body Boro is inhabiting was not originally his own but that of Jennifer, a typical suburban mom. In trying to explain their mother's absence of the past ten years to Jennifer's very confused, now teenage children, Boro says, "You know *this* body. You lived inside this body. Now I live inside it."

I keep going back to Boro's thought experiment. I try to image what I would be if I was a house. Would I be the creepy, deserted-looking house on the block? Is that what I want to be or what I am, and what does that say about me? I think my exterior is more Holda, but my interior is too messy for that. It's a cluttered and cobwebbed Victorian mansion one day, a minimal brutalist compound the next. I wonder, if someone wanted to hurt me, what would they break?

My final witch house is real, and the women who lived there were not actually witches, but they were enchanting. The house was everything one would imagine an inhabited haunted space to be. The structure might be decaying but those who reside there are very much alive. A place where sweaters are head scarves and skirts are capes, where there's always music playing. A house where the pâté might be cat food, but there's always ice cream.

Un-Domesticated

"At Grey Gardens, the world cannot intrude. With no formality of conduct, convention, or customs, the old house slowly envelops my mind and soul like a soft cocoon. Time seems not to exist, and the cats watch with interest. Only the raccoons live in reality, in the now."

— *My Life at Grey Gardens: 13 Months and Beyond. A True and Factual Book*, Lois Wright

"It must be fun to live in a house where you never have to clean up." In the 1972 *New York Magazine* article "The Secrets of Grey Gardens," Gail Sheehy recalls when her daughter met Little Edie Beale for the first time. She was not what the little girl was expecting. The shabby grey house her daughter called the Witch House was almost completely obscured by tall grass, bushes, and trees overgrown into each other, as if the earth were swallowing it whole. You would think it was abandoned except for the single light in the upstairs window and the gang of cats that roamed the property. But the woman who lived there was "not at all a proper witch. She looked sweet sixteen going on 30-odd and had carefully applied lipstick, eyeliner, and powder to her faintly freckled face."

She said to the girl, "Oh, Mother thinks it's artistic this way, like a Frank Lloyd Wright house. Don't you love the overgrown Louisiana Bayou look?" While it's not quite Falling Water, the house did look as though it was merging with the environment, just not by design. In 1976, the rest of the world got a look at the Witch House of East Hampton when filmmakers Albert and David Maysles released the brilliant and sometimes uncomfortably intimate documentary *Grey Gardens*. It was initially intended to be a movie about socialite Lee Radziwill, sister of former first lady Jacqueline Kennedy Onassis, and their summers in the Hamptons (which sounds insufferable if you ask me). Then Radziwill suggested her eccentric aunt with the beautiful singing voice do the narration, and the focus immediately shifted to the far more interesting Edith Beale, her daughter Edie, and their dilapidated, garbage-ridden mansion.

While the documentary is about Big and Little Edie, it's the house that gets top billing. The landscape architect gave it its moniker back in 1913, inspired by the soft grey of the dunes, the sea mist, and the pale climbing rose, lavender, phlox, and delphinium flowers enclosed by ornate concrete walls imported from Spain.[10] But even new, the name suggests an aging place, a place of lush color now dim, brittle, and old.

There is something terribly romantic about a house with a name in ruin. Old wealthy families have houses with names, second summer houses have names, and seeing one in this state exudes tragedy, like a wedding dress in a thrift store. The once-charming Gilded Age house in decay has the gothic quality of being simultaneously repulsive and riveting. The dried, dead vines crawling along the grey shingle-clad exterior, with its weathered, pale green window shutters and peeling paint, look haunting and sad. When we see Edie, bright, open, and teasingly flirtatious with the filmmakers in her DIY revolutionary costume, her energy doesn't match that of the house, and that dissonance carries through the film. When Edie says the house "is oozing with romance, ghosts, and other things," she is perfectly aware of the state of decay, like a ghost giving a tour of its own haunted house.

Grey Gardens is on a dead-end street where Lily Pond Lane meets West End Road in the village of East Hampton, what Little Edie calls "a mean, nasty, Republican Town."[11] The Hamptons consists of a series of coastal hamlets and villages in Long Island, and it has long been a vacation destination for wealthy New Yorkers. But in the 1950s and '60s, the Hamptons was a haven for artists; Andy Warhol, Peter Beard, Jackson Pollock, Lee Krasner, Willem and Elaine de Kooning, to name a few. For Edith, who dreamed of becoming a singer (to the embarrassment of her husband and father), living in a bohemian enclave was a natural fit. But by the 1970s the artists were moving out and the wealthy moved in, and the Beales' strange, "artistic" sensibilities were not appreciated. As Little Edie said, "They'll get you in East Hampton for wearing red shoes on a Thursday."[12]

Phelan Beale bought the 1897 Arts and Crafts summer cottage for his wife Edith in 1923. When they separated in 1934, the summer getaway became Edith's permanent home. She received money for child support for a while, but no alimony. Disapproving of her arty friends and bohemian lifestyle, her father disowned her, and without the financial means to keep up the estate, it rapidly fell into ruin. Meanwhile, her daughter Edie was trying to make a go of it in New York. After a brief modeling/acting/singing career, Little Edie moved back home at the age of thirty-five, where she would become an emotionally captive caretaker and companion for her mother for the next twenty-five years. As their trust fund incomes dwindled away, Grey Gardens fell apart around them. The garbage accumulated, the stench carried, their property became more and more of an eyesore, and the people of East Hampton were starting to complain.

Grey Gardens begins with the Beales speculating that Whiskers the cat has escaped through a raccoon-sized hole in the upper corner of the hallway, ruining the freshly painted blue wall. Looking out of the front door, Little Edie predicts they'll be raided again. It's happened before. The Suffolk County Health Department had threatened the Beales with eviction and in 1971, they followed through, taking all the cats and blasting the interior of their home with water hoses. When the press swooped in, lured by the proximity to American royalty and the spectacle of a reversal of fortune, the world was introduced to the Beales. The *New York Post* called their home "a garbage-ridden, filthy 28-room house with eight cats, fleas, cobwebs, and no running water."[13] The documentary opens with a still image of newspaper clippings with headlines reading "Mother and daughter ordered to clean up or get out," and "Mansion of filth." The photos accompanying Sheehy's article show Little Edie holding a cat in front of a waist-high pile of empty cans, sitting elegantly in a dismal room with stained floors, deteriorating walls, and furniture coated with dust. Jackie put in $30,000 to get the place fixed up enough to pass inspection, and as shocking as the state of the house is in the documentary, this was after the renovations and repairs. In the film, most of the activity happens in the bedroom that mother and daughter share; side-by-side twin beds are covered in old photographs, papers, and records wrapped in newspaper, but the walls are newly painted a fresh, bright yellow.

While it may exacerbate the codependency of their relationship and add to the strangeness of their dynamic, their reasons for spending much of their life in the same room are not as bizarre as they are practical. Unable to afford to heat the whole house, the bedroom was one of the few warm areas. In her old age, Big Edie's mobility was declining and she hated being alone, so it was easier for her daughter to keep an eye on her. The accumulation of debris that cluttered their home may have been a sign of syllogomania (trash hoarding), but there was more to the story. The city of East Hampton required residents to pay for garbage collection and often the Beales simply did not have the extra money. The brilliant remixing of Little Edie's clothes and head scarves were both a way to hide her alopecia and sheer creativity due to lack of funds.

By the end of filming, the raccoon/cat-sized hole in the corner has expanded to a third of the entire wall from floor to ceiling. A small fire broke out in the gap, probably due to faulty wiring, and in a panic Edie grabbed a blanket to smother the flames, one given to them by Jackie O., worth about $1400.

The city considered them demented, pathetic creatures. East Hampton acting mayor William Abel described them as two mentally incompetent "sweet old things." They were called recluses, regardless of the fact they had visitors and often talked to relatives and friends on the phone. There were people who helped them: gardener and handy man Brooks Hyers; their friend Lois Wright, who lived there for a spell; Tom Logan, a previous caretaker who died sleeping on a cot in the kitchen (his ghost is believed to haunt the place); and the famous grocery delivery boy Jerry "Marble Fawn" Torree. They were not alone or isolated. Being at odds with the world around them does not mean they were disengaged from it.

The state of their home may suggest mental illness, senility, or incapacitation, but it can also be seen as an act of defiance of a world that insisted on conformity and bland uniformity, and as resistance to the belief that women like them were supposed to project restraint, perfection, and quiet compliance. In the film we see a cat urinating behind a portrait of Big Edie leaning against the wall, to which she said, "I'm glad somebody's doing something they want to do." The Beales weren't crazy. They didn't give a fuck and that made a lot of people uncomfortable.

There is the knee-jerk instinct to diagnose and pathologize them: schizophrenia, senility, toxoplasmosis (the cat lady disease), syllogomania, senile squalor syndrome, or Diogenes syndrome (a catch-all term for a myriad of issues: hoarding garbage, domestic squalor. The term refers to the ancient Greek philosopher Diogenes the Cynic, "renowned for living without shame in self-chosen poverty"[14]). The Beales are completely and gloriously shameless. We might find their home (particularly pre-Jackie) disturbing, repulsive even. To leave one's home and possessions to rot suggests a withdrawal from life, a decline in capacity, but I prefer to think of their inertia as a state of what Scott Herring calls "material noncompliance." We expect miserable people to live in miserable conditions. We expect the once wealthy to have a reverence for materiality. We expect them to hide in the dark, but they invited a documentary crew into their home to film them in their most vulnerable moments. We would expect sadness and a lot less singing, dancing, and costume changes. We don't expect that much life in a dying space, but they reminisce, listen to the radio, chat with Jerry, bicker, read horoscopes, feed the cats, eat ice cream, cook corn on the cob in bed, recite poetry, and sing. They sing a lot. Little Edie often speaks of wanting to leave. She missed the noise of New

York City and hated the silence of the country. But she doesn't talk about wanting to escape the house, just the Hamptons.

Grey Gardens is a liminal place where time has stopped for the inhabitants yet marches on for the house. Housework is about maintaining what exists, keeping things from aging, to keep the illusion that time has not passed. We sweep the dust, we fix the crack in the wall, we repair, clean, refresh, and replace with the hope of sustaining newness as long as possible. As Iris Marion Young says, "The act of housework is an attempt to 'perpetuate the present,'" so it seems fitting that the Beales are not so concerned with being maintained. As Edie says, "It's very difficult to keep the line between the past and the present."

In the mockumentary television series *Documentary Now* episode "Sandy Passage," Fred Armisen and Bill Hader play Big and Little Vivvy Van Klimpton, in a pitch-perfect recreation of *Grey Gardens*. It takes all the cliches we have about the fear of aging and turns them into an actual horror movie. The episode is a faithful re-enactment with only slight exaggeration, as documentarians Larry and Abraham Fein film Little Vivvy feeding the cats bowls of Corn Flakes topped with slices of bologna as Big Vivvy sits in bed stirring a gin and tonic in a fishbowl. But throughout the episode, there are hints of something darker lurking in the dusty corners. When they find Barry, their loyal grocery delivery boy, chained up in a basement closet, the show turns into pure horror. Big Vivvy lurches after Larry, teeth bared as Abraham runs through the house, finding a wall covered with images of his brother and with "Mrs. Vivvy Fein" scrawled all over it. He runs past a bathtub full of snakes, while outside the smiling gardener is digging two graves. It ends with a title card reading, "The Fein Brothers were never seen again." The episode plays with our discomfort with the Beale's house; it takes the rumors and allegations about them and blows them up to absurd proportions. If you all think they're weird, you don't know the half of it. You thought they were just a couple of helpless old cat ladies, but watch your back. In case you didn't know, you're dealing with some staunch characters.

Gail Sheehy's daughter called Grey Gardens a "witch house" because it's what we associate with houses like this. Decay is scary, and you must be a little spooky to want to live in it. But it gets to the heart of what a witch house represents. It serves a different purpose beyond housekeeping and homemaking. A witch home is made for the witch. It serves only the witch and her needs and desires, and she does whatever she wants inside of it. Whether we like it or not.

Big Edie Beale died in 1977, two years after the release of the documentary. Two years after that, Little Edie sold Grey Gardens to writer Sally Quinn on the condition that she restore it to its original state. Despite the cat shit on the walls, the raccoons peering through the caved in ceiling, and the dirt floors, Quinn thought "it was the prettiest house I had ever seen"[15] Showing her around, Edie cheekily did a spin and said, "All it needs is a coat of paint!" During the walkthrough, Quinn touched a key on a grand piano in the living room, and it collapsed through the floor.

My favorite photo of the Beales is of the two women peering through the screen door: Big Edie, with flowing white hair, glasses, big bauble earrings, and wide eyes cast to the right with a mischievous grin; Little Edie looks suspicious and serious. Her signature headscarf pinned with a broach blends into the darkness. Her face is luminous and seems to float in the air. They both look amused and defiant.

As an eleven-year-old, Edie kept a diary documenting every day of 1929, and on the first page, in strong capital letters, she wrote, "I ONLY MARK THE HOURS THAT SHINE." Perhaps that is why time moves at a different pace at Grey Gardens: they only choose the moments that shine, dismissing the ones that are dim.

Staunch Houses

There is one house in America that is officially called "The Witch House," and that's the Corwin House in Salem, Massachusetts, the former home of Judge Jonathan Corwin (1640–1718). It seems insulting to call it that, since Corwin was the judge who signed the arrest warrant for Bridget Bishop, one of the nineteen innocent people executed during the Salem witch trials. As the only structure left with a direct connection to the trials, the house is a must-see destination for tourists, with hundreds of thousands of visitors a year — its peak season being Halloween, of course. Built in 1665, the house is a prime example of typical seventeenth-century New England architecture. The black exterior may look appropriately ominous, but it was typical back then, as is the famous House of Seven Gables just a mile away, but there's nothing particularly witchy about it.

I know a witch house when I see one, and it often has nothing to do with magical powers. In *Auntie Mame* (1958), the décor of the titular character's luxury Manhattan duplex apartment seems to miraculously shift styles from Chinese, Twenties Modern, Postmodern Neoclassical, English, Danish Modern, to East Indian following the twists and turns of her avant-garde life of hedonistic parties with artists, free thinkers, and bulldaggers.

Mame's house is a witch house. The *Bewitched* house on Morning Glory Circle is not a witch house. Samantha Stephens uses her power surreptitiously, hiding or disavowing her magic for the sake of her husband. I don't know where her loud and proud witch of a mother lived, but I bet Endora's house was a witch house.

Depictions of the witch house, even at its most cartoonish, as something old, decrepit, and uninviting, are commentaries not so much on building style as on expectations of how women are to live and how they are to age. More often than not, what we think of as a witch house is an architectural manifestation of the crone, the hag, or the spinster. Despite the fact that more women are choosing not to marry or have children, there is still a stigma attached to the cis-gendered, straight woman who is able to have children but doesn't want to, or who isn't married and doesn't want to be. The rise of "trad-wife" TikTok videos, the proliferation of Andrew Tate-ist influencer misogyny, and in America, the loss of our Constitutional right to abortion are all evidence that the fear of aging female autonomy is still a real thing. In the 2023 horror movie *The Clock*, the idea of a woman not wanting to have children is seen as a disease to be cured; with the right treatment, any woman can be driven to long for motherhood, no matter how horrific the therapy.

There is still a prevailing attitude that a single, childless woman living alone is something of an aberration and a condition to avoid, at best, and one to fear, at worst. But as Mona Chollet writes, "The witch embodies a woman free of all domination, all limitation; she is an ideal to aim for; she shows us the way."[16] The witch doesn't fear being maligned or demonized or ostracized. Her house is a centralized manifestation of power that challenges our perception of old women who choose to live alone. The witch house couldn't care less what you think.

Mad Houses

Ted's House

"If architecture is the art of enclosing space for a purpose, Kaczynski's house warns us not to seek that space, not to go inside, not to be too curious for what is or was within."

— Richard Ford, "Evil's Humble Home."
New York Times Magazine, 1998

In E.T.A. Hoffmann's short story *The Cremona Violin*, the narrator begins "Councillor Krespel was one of the strangest, oddest men I ever met within my life." Krespel, the eccentric diplomat/polymath/violin maker, is obsessive about all things, and music in particular. He collects rare violins, but only plays them once before breaking them apart to figure out how they're made. His daughter Antonia sings with such sublime beauty that he's compelled to lock her away, forbidding her to sing for anyone other than himself. However, our introduction to Krespel is not through music but through architecture and his very unusual approach to designing his house. Instead of a floorplan, Krespel draws a square-shaped trench in the ground and tells his builders, "Here's where you must lay the foundations; then carry up the walls until I say they are high enough." They think it's a bit weird, but he's filling them up with food and booze, so they don't question their boss's methodology. Once the walls are up, he peruses their work, "… running his sharp nose hard against the wall, he cried, "Come here, come here, men! Break me a door in here! Here's where I want a door made!"

Once inside, he walks through the space, the bricklayers behind him with hammers and picks at the ready wherever he cries, "Make a window here, six feet high by four feet broad! There, a little window, three feet by two!" Driven by some instinctual urge, he directs his workers to knock out windows wherever it feels right. On the outside it may look irrational, but "the interior arrangements suggested a peculiar feeling of comfort." Krespel's house is as unique and specific to him as a fingerprint. It's a house designed from the inside out, its windows positioned for one person's singular point of view.

The windows of the Unabomber cabin bother me. So does the door. It seems proportionately a bit too tall for its width, like a mathematically correct dimension based on the Golden Rule or Fibonacci sequence or some other classical theorem, but it doesn't look right. There's no window in the back. There's a small square window on each side, one in a place you would expect a window to be, the other positioned right underneath the eave, right up to near the top. It's awkward and too high. One window is right above the desk with a view of the access road. The other view reveals just the sky. The windows are small, meant for only one head at a time, on the inside, looking out. They are windows for someone who doesn't particularly need a lot of sunlight, or who doesn't want people looking in. It's as if someone sat down at the desk, in front of the typewriter, and like Krespel, traced a square on the wood in front of him and punched out a window. I can't speculate as to how much thought he gave to how many windows he would have and where they should be. I don't think aesthetics were his primary concern in the creation of his cabin, but there is an obsessive precision about its silhouette that I find disturbing for reasons I'm not exactly sure of. It's just a feeling.

In 1971, Ted Kaczynski and his brother David bought a 1.4-acre plot on Bald Mountain near the Blackfoot River in Montana, where Ted would build his 10x12' house out of repurposed plywood from an abandoned cabin. The size of his house is about the same as his exemplar Henry David Thoreau's cabin on Walden Pond, but Thoreau only spent two years in his cabin. Ted would be in his for twenty-five. Henry had visitors and threw parties at his place, and the windows were much, much bigger.

After Ted's arrest on 3 April, 1996, the cabin was emptied of two decades worth of belongings turned evidence. Without the books, journals, typewriter, snowshoes, oatmeal and baking soda canisters repurposed as bomb-making materials, the pots, pans, guns, the zither by the door, and the assortment of aviator glasses, the cabin is left a grimy wooden shell. It was removed from its little patch of land in the woods for safekeeping from vandals and souvenir hunters and stored in a nearby air base, until its big move in December of 1997. It was placed on its side on a flatbed truck and covered with a tarp as if it had laid down to sleep through the long 1,100-mile journey from Lincoln, Montana, to Sacramento, California. After a seventeen-year reign of terror, the country finally got a look at the Unabomber and the tiny cabin that came to represent the man and his manifesto.

In one photograph on the website of SafeStore USA — the company charged with transporting the cabin — a few people are gathered around the cabin after it had been loaded onto the truck. A reporter holds a microphone to a man and woman next to him, but it oddly looks as if he's holding the mic to the cabin, hoping for a quote, to get some insider information on the thing that knew Ted best. I see Ted's cabin as an unwilling accomplice. How was the cabin to know what Ted would be doing inside? The wood Ted used had a life before him, maybe as a fishing shack for long weekend get-aways, a pottery studio, or simply just storage. It's not the cabin's fault, don't blame it.

Unabomber Cabin, Newseum (2019), author photo

In the Discovery Channel series *Manhunt: The Unabomber* (2017), the cabin is sawed off from the stakes, strapped down, and lifted by helicopter, spinning through the air like an oversized Monopoly piece. It is the perfect silhouette of a house in its most reduced and perfect form. In reality, the decision to airlift the cabin was broached and ultimately vetoed, but it makes a dramatic image, this modest, little shack elevated to a totem of isolation, a single delicate thing dangling precariously over the streets of Lincoln.

The cabin was introduced in the trial by Ted's own defense team, who hoped that it would convince the jury of his insanity once they could see it and step inside his tiny, tiny world. Attorney Dennis Wacks said, "We want to show how [life in the cabin] affected his mental state. I think once (jurors) see all the evidence in all its totality, they'll see that Mr. Kaczynski had some psychological problems." Defense attorney Quin Denvir added, "While jurors are often taken to crime scenes in trials in this case, it was easier to bring the view to the jury." [1]

One detail in particular was brought to the jury's attention. There was no doorknob on his front door, just three padlocks. The defense hoped this little detail would be indicative of his paranoia, but my first apartment in New York City had three locks and a chain, so this isn't so weird to me. Even the size of his cabin was about the same square-footage as my room in that apartment. But the lack of a doorknob got to me. It's something I never thought much about before, the symbolic nature of it. Without it, the cabin is a bit less of a home. It falls into the "shack" category: somewhere to store objects, not to house people. It's not the number of locks on the door, but the refusal to even have such a small gesture of accessibility, this symbolic handshake inviting you into a place. Equally, it's not the smallness of his home that reveals psychopathy, but the lack of humanity, as if material simplicity was antithetical to personality. In all the grubby clutter, there was not one photograph, postcard, or image of a painting cut out of a magazine. Nothing to signify that a human being lived there. It is a space for a singular purpose that had little concern for life.

Once the cabin arrived at the warehouse in California, photographer Richard Barnes was the only journalist allowed inside. Writer Leah Worthington notes that *The New York Times* "wanted to see any architectural work in his portfolio, particularly of warehouses, though they wouldn't explain why."[2] The cabin sat flat on the concrete floor instead of suspended on posts embedded in the earth. It was framed by metal support beams and exposed pipes instead of tree branches, and the room flooded with stark fluorescents instead of filtered sunlight.

Contained inside solid white walls and shot at a three-quarter view, the cabin could have been in an art gallery in Chelsea, an exhibit at MoMA. It stopped being a home and became an artifact, a symbol, a metaphor for something else.

Next was a series of black-and-white "portraits," with each side shot straight on (the interior was off limits to him). Barnes draped the walls of the warehouse in black, so the cabin appears as an artifact without reference to size or scale. It's a specimen. Each detail is in sharp focus; the grain of the wood, each precisely hammered nail. Twice removed from context, out of the woods, out of the warehouse/gallery, out of physical space entirely, the cabin floats in a void, in nothingness.

Barnes' *Press Conference with Cabin* (2004) is like the SafeStore USA photo. The cabin is outside, facing a crowd of photographers, video cameras, and reporters. With the door removed, it appears open mouthed, preparing to make a statement. The cabin poses for the paparazzi, taking its moment in the spotlight without that diva Ted soaking up all the attention before its next destination, where we would finally meet, in Washington, D.C.

The Unabomber cabin was the star of the *G-Men and Journalists: Top News Stories of the FBI's First Century* exhibit at the now closed Newseum. There you could see the coat Patty Hearst wore when she robbed a bank with the Symbionese Liberation Army, a collection of crushed and dust-coated cell phones and pagers from the World Trade Center rubble, and a piece of rope used to climb into the Lindbergh baby's bedroom. But Ted's old house is the showstopper in the section titled "A Mad Bomber and His Manifesto."

I went to the awkwardly named and even more awkwardly

conceived Newseum as soon as they announced it was closing, since it would be, in all likelihood, my only opportunity to see the cabin before it went back into whatever storage facility the FBI uses to store houses. It's disarming in person, almost cute. The ceiling of the museum space wasn't very high, and the cabin fit comfortably in a corner of the room. There were panels with other artifacts — newspaper clippings, the infamous police sketch, yellowed pages of the original *Industrial Society and its Future* — above a cutout through the little square window allowing one to peer inside, an experience Ted never would have allowed. Through the doorway you can examine the empty cabin and its walls of bare shelves. There's a black Ted-sized stain against the wall where he slept for twenty-five years on a plywood board covered with a thin layer of foam. It's a bit pathetic (like Kaczynski himself) and terribly lonely. There's a small barrier blocking entry with a sign reading "Do Not Touch the Unabomber Cabin." Like a good museum-goer, I respect archival objects, so I didn't. Before my visit I contacted the curator of the museum, asking if I would be able to enter the cabin for research purposes. In less than an hour, I received a terse and unequivocal "No." I forget sometimes that it's not just a house; it's evidence.

Before his death in 2023, Ted lived for twenty-five years (the same length of time as in his cabin) in a 12x7' cell in a supermax prison in Florence, Colorado; about the same size as his cabin, just a slightly different proportion. Kaczynski wasn't insane because he chose to live in a cabin. It seemed an unnecessary and dramatic gesture to haul out the house, one coming from a privileged position. All sorts of people all over the world live in very small spaces, whether it's their culture or their conditions. All sorts of people live off the grid, sometimes because they want to and sometimes because they have no choice. The defense team could count on an American jury of consumers, conditioned to desire *more*, to believe that needing or wanting less (less money, less space, less stuff) is tantamount to madness. Kaczynski had a laundry list of emotional, social, and psychological problems, but living in a cabin wasn't one of them.

Just to be clear, I don't give a shit about Ted Kaczynski. I don't think the fact that he might have had a few good points about the insidious hold technology has on our lives makes up for the fact that he murdered random, innocent people and hoped to murder a lot more. But I do think that houses retain some of the emotional human residue of their former inhabitants (and in Ted's case, a lot of physical residue). Perhaps that is why his cabin fascinates me, and why Barnes' photos are so haunting. That much violence, bitterness, rage, loneliness, and spite, concentrated in such a small container, must leave something soaked in the wood. His house has always been more interesting to me than the man.

Ted Kaczynski relinquished his right to privacy and seclusion when he mailed his first bomb. He lost ownership of his beloved cabin when he was led away in handcuffs and taken into FBI custody. On the train back to New York from D.C., I immediately regretted my obedience to that little sign blocking the entrance. So the next weekend I went back, and I touched it.

Norman's House

"In this house the most dire, horrible events took place. I think we can go inside because the place is up for sale. Although I don't know who's going to buy it now."

— *Alfred Hitchcock's Tour of the Psycho Set*, 1960

Edward Hopper was the master of capturing isolation and estrangement on canvas: a solitary businessman looking out of the window from a desk; a woman in a coat and hat alone at a cafe table; an usher in a movie theater waiting in the wings. But his paintings of houses are just as evocative of that loneliness, even without people. In Hopper's *House by the Railroad* (1925), a large Second Empire Revival house sits isolated on a hill. With no other houses or trees, and with nothing else in the landscape, the house is eerie in its solitude. Positioned at a three-quarter view, our gaze is slightly upward. The cool blues and greys of the house are contrasted with the rusty orange of train tracks that cut across the front. The house is a remnant of a golden age that died long ago, and the world is passing it by.

Edward Hopper, *House by the Railroad* (1925),
The Metropolitan Museum of Art

Psycho (1960), Alfred Hitchcock

Sometimes Hopper includes a figure in the windows of his house portraits, or a light on in a room, a suggestion of human life. There are no such indicators in *House by the Railroad*. But in Alfred Hitchcock's *Psycho* (1960), the silhouette of a feminine figure with her hair pulled back in a bun walks past the second-floor window while a woman waits in her car below, hoping for a room to rent for the night. Our view of the Bates House is from the same perspective as in *House by the Railroad*, looking up at a three-quarter view at the top of a hill, distant and foreboding.

When Marion Crane (Janet Leigh) arrives, the Bates Motel is completely vacant; typical for them since the highway was moved, a fate common to mom-and-pop roadside motels across America. Marion thinks she might have gotten off the main road, and Norman (Anthony Perkins) says, "I knew you must have. No one stops here anymore unless they do."

The house and the motel are places you pass by on your way somewhere else, not somewhere to stop.

Hitchcock used *House by the Railroad* as the reference point for Norman Bates' house, or rather his mother's house (or even more accurately, probably his grandmother's house). If the Bates house was real (it wasn't, only the front and side façades were built on the backlot of Universal Studios), it would have been built sometime between 1855 and 1885, and the Bates family would have been rather well off. The Second Empire style, borrowed from the French during the reign of Napoleon III, is characterized by its sloping, slate shingle mansard roofs with spiky iron work, ornamental wood trim, shadowy verandas, and imposingly large eaves. It was, at the time, a sign of wealth and opulence, but after the financial panic of 1873, the grandiosity of huge, frosted houses began to look a bit vulgar. By the crash of 1929 and the Great Depression, they were laughable. What had been the height of elegance became ostentatious and the Gilded Age was tarnished. No one was living in Hopper's house after that railroad arrived.

As the formerly stately mansions aged, as its inhabitants died off, all those embellishments and spiky details went from fancy to creepy, and the Second Empire mansion with the mansard roof was fully cemented as the traditional architecture of the American gothic. The model Shirley Jackson used for *The Haunting of Hill House* was also in the "gingerbread house" style, with "an air of disease and decay."[3] The Victorian house with its antiquated ornamentation was a dying breed, representing the pre-war, pre-Modernist aesthetic of inherited wealth and the glorification of old-world European style. All that curlicue embellishment allowed for too many places for dust to accumulate, cobwebs to hang, and weird shadows to be cast in a candlelit room. Those top-heavy tower rooms were perfect for locking away family secrets and regrettable choices. Dripping with filigree, it's a style that is both whimsical and threatening, absurd and imposing. By the 1920s, the image of the ideal home had returned to something simpler: the cleaner and minimal Colonial, "an all-out revival in domestic architecture, representing something pure, and purely American, rooted in the traditions of early (and infinitely more virtuous) American home life." [4] The Bates Motel is Colonial.

The motel is the younger of the two domains in Norman's world, and the one where he is in control. It's the world where he can welcome guests, make conversation with strangers, and where he is almost charming. It is his place of comfort, where he has his peep hole in the office wall to spy on whomever he assigns room number one. But the parlor where he and Marion chat over sandwiches has a touch of the Victorian: a bit claustrophobic, cluttered with stuffed dead things and grandmother-y knick-knacks. Just as Norman dresses in his mother's clothes and slips into her identity, the house is another skin for him to inhabit. The house dominates the landscape just as his mother dominates Norman, and the motel is no match for such an imposing figure. In the house, Norman's bedroom is a child's room, with toys and stuffed animals on the shelves and an unmade twin bed, locked in an infantilized state. In the motel he's a grown man. In the house, he is his mother's child.

With its oversized sloping roofs, the house is a vertical mass jutting up out of the hill, like a stuffed bird of prey hovering over the motel, poised to strike. The motel's flat, single-floor spread is meek in comparison, lying prostrate on the concrete below. The contrast between the two structures is almost absurd. Despite its comparative youth, the mid-century motel is just as desolate as the Victorian mansion on the hill, both icons of modernity in their respective eras now architectural relics, "dead structures facing an isolated future."[5]

As the American freeway system expanded in the 1930s and '40s, and as car ownership exploded in the '50s, more Americans were driving across the country for leisure, and they needed convenient places to stay along the way. Motels were safe, inexpensive, and a clean resting place for a family road trip to Mt Rushmore. But by the time the Interstate Highway System was established in 1956, those quaint little cottages were bypassed, and big chain Holiday Inns were taking their place. Motels would gain another reputation, as places for illicit sex, secret affairs, or as temporary hide-outs for people on the run.

The Addams Family (1964)

Shortly after *Psycho*, the Second Empire style made its appearance again in the home for *The Addams Family* (1964), and what was once intimidating and imposing became the architecture of Halloween decorations and *Scooby-Doo* cartoons. Even in *Beetlejuice* (1988), Charles and Delia Deetz's deconstructed Connecticut house on the hill keeps the tell-tale mansard roof. In Greta Gerwig's *Barbie* (2023), Weird Barbie's House is a wacky, minimalist modern structure (with open walls like all Dream Houses), at the top of a hill at the end of a winding staircase. It's a long, flat trapezoid with a tower extending out of the top with a minimal stylized mansard roof, a plastic pop version of the *Psycho* house, fitting for the strangest Barbie in Barbieland.

The house has made its way into the fine arts as well. From April to October 2016, the Bates' house appeared on the roof of the Metropolitan Museum of Art in New York. Artist Cornelia Parker's *Transitional Object (PsychoBarn)* was a thirty-foot-tall recreation of the Bates' house with the glimmering Manhattan skyline as its backdrop. It was disorienting to see this famous house of horror in such an unlikely place, under even more unlikely circumstances, as I drank white wine and watched the orange-pink sunset over Central Park. Like the *Psycho* house, only the front and right façade were constructed, but it didn't matter. We've only ever known the house from that ¾ view, it's all we need to see. Made at two-thirds scale, the house is too small to be real and too big to be a playhouse, it's a strange, stunted proportion. In psychoanalysis, a transitional object is something a child clings to during the weaning stage: a teddy bear, a blanket. It provides a comforting stability during that tricky time between being one with mother and being an independent being, a safety net from the breast to the bottle. Norman never made that crossing, he never transitioned.[6]

But there was something a bit too *warm* about this construction, not only because it's only ever appeared in black and white, but because of its material: salvaged wood from an old red farmhouse in Upstate New York destined for demolition. One architectural icon made from the dying parts of another. The solitary *House by the Railroad*, the obsolete Bates motel, and the dilapidated classic red barn are all representatives of an abandoned and isolated American landscape, like the barn's accompanying structure: the farmhouse.

Ed's House

"You boys don't want to go messing around no old house now; those old things is dangerous. You liable to get hurt."
— *The Texas Chainsaw Massacre*, 1974

The first time I visited Kansas it was for my grandmother's funeral. A family friend picked me up from the airport (which is in Kansas City, Missouri, not Kansas City, Kansas) and as he drove, the highway cut through an expanse of wheat on either side. It was a good hour of nothing but amber waves of grain on either side when suddenly he made a sharp turn right and we were *in it*, inside of the heart of the heartland, through the wheat, across a little bridge and into the city of Atchison, birthplace of Amelia Earhart. I had never seen the plains at ground level before. Most of this part of the country I'd seen from 35,000 feet as a patchwork quilt of browns, tans, and greens divided into squares measured in acres. As someone who has spent most of her life in apartments, it was a bit thrilling. And a smidge creepy in a *Children of the Corn* kind of way.

The Bender family farmhouse in Labette County, Kansas, is miniscule compared to the space around it. The little two room house sits on 160 acres, and considering the number of people who lived in it, and the number of people who died in it, the house is disturbingly small. There is a vast amount of nothingness around the Bender homestead; there isn't a single tree as far as the eye can see, just an ocean of low grass. Photographs in faded sepia show the rundown clapboard house with boards missing, leaving long gashes along the side. There is another photo, the house further in the distance, a group of men gathered in front of a series of misaligned rectangular holes in the ground and three oblong, plain wooden boxes beside them. It was there they found eleven bodies, all travelers making their way West along the Great Osage Trail, who made the mistake of stopping by the Benders'.

In 1871, John Bender, his wife Elvira, their son (they think) John Jr, and their daughter Kate (who may have been John Jr's lover, no one is quite sure), immigrated from Germany (it's believed but no one is sure of that either) to claim their bit of land as part of the Homestead Act. In an effort to encourage western expansion, eight million acres of land were stolen from the Osage and distributed by the federal government to anyone with the $18 claimant fee. If you pledged to stay five years and do something productive with the land, it was yours to keep. It's safe to say the Benders were not very productive.

Death was their livelihood, in more ways than one. Unsuspecting customers hoping for a message from the other side came for Kate's services as a medium. There was a meager dry goods shop where someone passing through could buy some supplies, a bed if someone needed a place to rest, and a meal if they were hungry. This 16x24' house functioned as a home for a family of four, a general store, a séance room, and the world's most depressing bed and breakfast all in one. And there were flies everywhere.

Dividing the house between the public and private spaces was a nine-foot-high, stained canvas wagon cover. An 1884 illustration by Edmund Pearson shows a cross section of the house: on one side, a guest is seated at the table, being served a meal by a woman. On the other, a man has a hammer raised high above his head, about to strike down on the unsuspecting victim. If a visitor appeared to be wealthy, the Benders would give them a seat of honor at the table with their back to the curtain. After the blow, the victim's throat was slit and the body dropped into the cellar through a trap door. Later, under the cover of darkness, the body would be stripped and buried in the orchard. The Bender home was designed for a singular purpose and the comfort of the people who lived there came second.

THE HOME OF THE BENDERS.—THE MACHINERY OF MURDER.

The Home of the Benders: The Machinery of Murder, History, Romance, and Philosophy of Great American Crimes, by Frank Triplett, 1884"

People tended to go missing in that part of the world back then; the plains were a dangerous place, but enough people managed to escape the Benders to evoke suspicion. When a popular doctor was the latest to mysteriously vanish, the authorities were led to the Benders' farm, only to find it abandoned, with the uniquely vile scent of human decomposition coming from the cellar. Like the Unabomber cabin, the house was moved by authorities investigating the crime. Unable to easily excavate the cellar from inside the house, it was easier to shift the whole building, exposing the blood-soaked hole in the ground. The Benders were never found.

With no clear end and no clear beginning, the vast treeless open plains offer no protection. Susan Jonusas describes a harrowing escape by a woman seeking Kate's services: Fleeing the house, "the black gulf of the prairie opened up before her as she ran." At the sound of a gunshot, she dropped down into the grass and "felt for imperfections in the ground where she could hide but she knew she had to run."[7] The sublimity of open space offers its own special terror. There is no place to hide, no protection, and the only shelter is a single house with strangers who may or may not be hospitable. On the farm, no one can hear you scream.

In 2022, the new owners of the Grand Central Cafe in Kingsland, Texas, changed the name of their quaint farmhouse turned casual southern restaurant to Hooper's, in honor of the man who made it famous. Saved from imminent ruin, the abandoned two-story Victorian clapboard house was moved from its original location on Quick Hill Road in the little town of Round Rock, reassembled, and lovingly restored. Freshly painted bright white with pine-green gables, it looks like a charming slice of classic Americana. If it wasn't for the framed photos and memorabilia, you would have no idea it was the primary location for Tobe Hooper's *The Texas Chainsaw Massacre* (1974), one of the most influential horror movies ever made. There you can enjoy a Hitchhiker's Highball and a chicken fried steak in the same dining room where Grandpa sucked the blood from Sally Hardesty's finger as she screamed under a lampshade made of human faces.

In the film, the infamous Chainsaw house is not the first one we encounter. We learn from a radio news report and a gruesome display of a decomposing corpse (posed holding the head of another decomposing corpse) that someone has been robbing graves in the fictional town of Newt, Texas. Sally (Marilyn Burns), along with her friends Jerry (Allen Danziger), Pam (Teri McMinn), Kirk (William Vail), and her brother Franklin (Paul A. Partain), are on their way to her grandparents' hometown to see if their graves are among the desecrated.

Our first stop is the Hardesty house. Long abandoned, the exterior is nearly completely engulfed in vegetation. The paint is chipped and peeling, old bones hang from the eaves like grotesque wind chimes, and there's a strange assemblage of skulls and feathers on the porch, an ominous message or the remains of some ritual finished long ago. The interior is dark and dismal, the windows are shattered, there are holes in the walls and ceiling, and it looks like someone could go crashing through the floorboards at any moment. But seeing past the gloom, Sally warmly reminisces about her childhood in the house, fondly touching the faded and peeling wallpaper. Meanwhile, in another room, Jerry recoils from a writhing mass of spiders clumped into a corner of the wall. While this may not be the house of horrors they're about to encounter, it is disturbing and horrible in its own way.

Pam and Kirk leave the group to explore a nearby swimming hole, and hearing the rumble of a generator (a bit like the roar of a chainsaw), they discover another house, one that is obviously occupied. They approach from the rear, and despite the unusual number of abandoned cars, it looks as ordinary and unassuming as any other house, if perhaps a little worn and showing its age. But the porch is tidy and clean, welcoming enough that someone could feel comfortable knocking on the door and asking a stranger for a favor. Even when Kirk finds a human molar by the door, it doesn't stop him from entering the house on his own.

Like the Hardesty house, the blazing Texas sun doesn't penetrate inside, and the foyer is dark and gloomy. The only light comes from the open door illuminating the blood-red wall at the end of the hall, an open mouth or wound, decorated with taxidermized animal heads. Then, suddenly, Leatherface (Gunnar Hansen) emerges, massive with a stained apron and misshapen mask that doesn't quite fit his face, he brings Kirk down with a blow to the head, then another to stop his spastic twitching. He drags his kill up a small wooden ramp through the doorway, and with a loud crash, slams the sliding metal door shut. It is still shocking even though I've watched it dozens of times. It is silent, like the house would be. There's no non-diegetic music warning us ahead of time, and the whole event is less than a minute. But the thing I find most disturbing is the little wooden ramp, propped up against the doorframe and the metal sliding door. It's a domestic interpretation of an industrial space, the family's personal abattoir.

In the next scene, what might be one of the most iconic shots in all of horror, Pam, who had been waiting for Kirk outside on a swing, gets up and walks casually to the house. Shot from below, her shorts are bright red against the white of the house, framed by bright green trees and the sky is blue with puffy clouds. It is a decidedly "red, white, and blue" image and a stark contrast to what she's about to see and experience. Shot at a slightly wide angle, the house appears to grow larger, enveloping her as she gets closer.

Once inside, she hears something stirring in the parlor. She turns into the room to the right and stumbles into a nightmare: a loveseat constructed from bones like an ossuary; a floor coated in grey chicken feathers, bones, and skulls from a variety of species, including human. Disgusted, she pulls herself up, only to be caught from behind by Leatherface. She makes it out of the door, kicking and screaming as he pulls her back inside into the darkness. Unfortunately for the actors, production designer Bob Burns used real animal carcasses, feathers, and bones throughout the production. In the dinner scene, real sausages were injected with formaldehyde to keep them from rotting in the Texas heat. To maintain light continuity in the interiors, the windows were draped in black, sealing in the heat (it would get up to 115 degrees inside), the stench adding an extra layer of revulsion to the realism.

For generations, the Sawyer (aka Slaughter) family worked in the local slaughterhouse, perfecting the craft of killing cattle with a hammer. Then automation came and took their jobs and livelihoods, so they applied their skills to people, kidnapping their own livestock for meat and foraging for crafting materials in graveyards.

The Hardesty house, grey and brittle, like the bones, feathers, and detritus in the Sawyer's kitchen, is another corpse drying out in the sun. If the house represents the body, the homes in *The Texas Chainsaw Massacre* express any number of fears: of aging, decay, and abandonment. The Hardesty house is a "necrotic architecture,"[8] vacant of human habitation, but still reverberating with memories of the past, still existing, but unoccupied, dead for all intents and purposes yet still standing, "like a corpse, within which yet flicker animations of the spirit."[9] The perception of the Sawyer house from the outside is that it is occupied and alive but shouldn't be. The house is a living mask covering a carcass.

The real Hardesty house remained abandoned and eventually burned down in 1979, and the Sawyer house was host to a variety of tenants after *Chainsaw*. Owners came and went, but it was eventually abandoned and left to vandals, the elements, and horror buffs come to bear witness to the birthplace of the slasher movie. The house went the way of many farmhouses of its kind, succumbing to the decline of the family farm in the face of corporate agriculture and the flight of the young to better opportunities in the city; one of many dried, grey corpses of clapboard houses leaning drunkenly before their inevitable collapse. Zombie houses.

Threatened with demolition, in 1998 the *Texas Chainsaw* house was sold to a cinephile who recognized its iconic status. It was disassembled into seven pieces and moved to the Antlers Hotel in Kingsland, Texas, where it was refurbished to its original quaint condition and ironically became a family-friendly restaurant. New housing developments and office complexes now surround the area where the house once stood. Grass grows between the cracks of Quick Hill Road, where Sally escaped in the back of a pick-up truck laughing in hysterics as Leatherface spun around wielding his roaring chainsaw. The road was cut off by a highway, the same fate that would befall the Bates Motel.

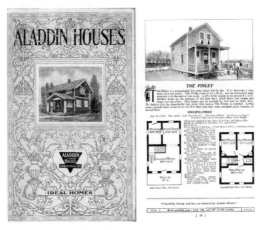

Aladdin Houses kit catalog, 1915

The real house playing the role of the fictional Sawyer Family homestead was built around 1909 and was one of many such houses across the country: an "L" shaped clapboard Queen Anne–style cottage you could literally buy from a catalog. Through companies like Sears, Montgomery Ward, Gordon-Van Tine, and Harris Homes, you could buy a kit house for as little as $450 (about $14,000 today), anything from a little one-bedroom bungalow to a grand three-story Colonial, customizable to fit your needs. Your new house would arrive by train in a boxcar with everything from the pre-cut lumber to the doorknobs, with the plans for assembly included like a gigantic IKEA flat pack.

It is the commonness of the *Chainsaw* house that is most disturbing. The utter trustworthy predictability of the exterior makes the interior and the activities within it so much more horrifying. It is a betrayal of our trust in standardized design. It's what led Pam and Kirk to assume that the house was a safe space, that the people who live there would be friendly and helpful. The banal quality of these homes is what Sorcha Ní Fhlainn refers to as "the terror of aesthetic normalcy." Quite literally anyone could have the same house anywhere in the country. An aberration as grotesque and impossible as a family of cannibals could happen anywhere, barely hidden behind any screen door: East Coast, West Coast, the South, or the Midwest, the kit house unified the identity of American houses everywhere. The *Psycho* house has none of that deception. It looks like "Mother," and it exudes exclusion and malevolence. It is a static house indicating generations of inherited wealth, not the new beginnings of a burgeoning middle class or the first-generation immigrant family. The *Addams Family* house is ostentatious in its otherness. The house *is* Morticia and Gomez, a perfect reflection of its gothic inhabitants; macabre and mysterious, with an eccentric dark romanticism. In comparison, the classic Sawyer farmhouse gives nothing away. It is an architecture able to mimic normalcy and pass for any other. As long as no one goes inside.

I couldn't say exactly when I heard about Ed Gein, but I can safely say that his house was the one that started me on this path. Unlike the creepy opulence of the Victorian mansion or the decayed castles of Medieval Europe, I could identify with Gein's house. I know his house. I have never lived on a farm or in the country, but I am genetically Midwestern: I've got Ohio and Michigan in me, plus some Indiana from my mother and Kansas from my father. The image of flat land broken with the silhouette of a modest house with one or two gabled shingled roofs and a covered porch in the distance feels familiar. While I never lived on a farm in the country or in a little house on the prairie, I still feel the warmth of recognition when I see them. Which is why it still fascinates me: how the origins of a horror archetype, the inspiration for Norman Bates, Leatherface, and Buffalo Bill, could have grown from such an ordinary house in such a mediocre landscape, a landscape where I could have come from.

Home of serial killer Ed Gein in Plainfield in Wisconsin in 1957,
Getty Images, Bettmann

No one had seen the inside of Ed Gein's house in a very long time, but in the 2 December, 1957, issue of *Life* magazine, the whole world got a look inside the unassuming, two-story, L-shaped farmhouse. There is a winter bleakness about the place, the bare branches of the trees and the thin layer of snow, tramped down by too many footsteps. There's nothing particularly interesting about it except perhaps for the uniformed police officer in front. There is one photo, taken from the inside of the house, of a man and woman outside, peeking through the widow, trying to see for themselves the living conditions of the Butcher of Plainfield, "through dirty, tattered curtains and past the cluttered sill into the kitchen." Like their neighbors, "all week, Plainfield's people came to see the house they had long ignored."[10]

If you were able to see through the dingy windows and into the gloom, you'd see a miserable, chaotic mess of junk and filth. Sad perhaps, kind of gross, maybe the abode of a borderline hoarder, but not unfathomable. But if you were one of the unfortunate members of the police department who entered the house, you'd have found a soup bowl made of a human skull, a window shade pull made from a pair of human lips, a chair seat made from human skin, human skulls set onto the bedposts, a belt made of nipples, pants made from human skin, and a vest made from a woman's torso. If you looked deeper into boxes and paper bags, you'd find a collection of vulvas in a box (one tied with a bow) and the face of fifty-one-year-old tavern owner Mary Hogan fashioned into a mask. Mary was the second murder Gein admitted to committing. He scavenged most of the body parts from local graveyards, scouring obituaries looking for recently deceased middle-aged women. He didn't have to confess to Bernice Worden's murder; she was the first thing police found on his property. In the shed, the body of fifty-eight-year-old Worden was hung upside down, split down the middle like a field-dressed deer, and decapitated. But back in the revolving hellscape of his house, if you managed to make it up to the second floor, you'd find Augusta Gein's room, his mother's room, untouched, locked away like a dusty shrine.

The Gein house sat on 150 acres of flat, infertile land outside of Plainfield, a part of the country author Harold Schechter describes as "oppressive in its emptiness."[11] The isolation of the house suited Augusta. Far away from the wanton harlots of Plainfield, she could sit on the porch with her adult sons at her knee, reciting Bible passages and instructing them on how to masturbate so they wouldn't be tempted by actual women. Ed's alcoholic and passive father had died of heart failure in 1940, then four years later his older brother Henry died under somewhat suspect circumstances in a brush fire (fires don't tend to leave strangle marks). But only a year later, Augusta had a debilitating stroke and died, leaving a devastated Ed all alone. For the first time in his life, at the age of thirty-nine, Ed had the house to himself.

Robert Bloch wrote *Psycho* after reading a newspaper article about Ed Gein. A year later Alfred Hitchcock would be given a copy to read, and the rest is horror movie history: Gein begat Norman Bates, who begat Leatherface, who begat Buffalo Bill. Ed's house mysteriously burned down to the relief of Plainfield, but the town is forever tainted as the hometown of the most infamous ghoul in the country.

To the folks in Plainfield, Ed's house evoked a spooky aura, and while no one knew the depth of the depravity happening inside, it was still best to avoid it. Especially at night, when "the only light to be seen from Eddie's house was the somber glow of an oil lamp behind his moldering kitchen curtains."[12] There is a Midwestern respect for privacy that worked to Ed's advantage: your business is your business, and what you do behind closed doors is no concern to anyone else. Gein was generally thought to be a little odd, but harmless. The creeping ill ease the people of Plainfield felt was reserved for the house, as if it was more polite to think of the building as being evil instead of the man who babysat their kids and ate pork chops and pickles at their table. If they didn't suspect Ed, they suspected his house. The amount of death, decay, and human debasement on that property must have radiated through the walls. When a neighbor was forced to walk past Ed's house after dark, he would sprint past as fast as he could. He wasn't scared of Ed. No one was. It wasn't Ed he was running from: "I feared the house."[13]

Sarah's House

"In this great house, there is no adherence to design anywhere. Large windows, small windows, round windows, square windows, lead windows, and windows of art glass are all in great conglomeration."

— "The 'Spirit House' of San Jose," *Oakland Tribune*, 29 October, 1922

If Ed's house was deceptively normal, Sarah's house was delightfully not. Where the previous examples of traditional homes hid the deviance of their inhabitants, this house wore its madness on its sleeve, but its owner was perfectly sane.

When Sarah Winchester moved to San Jose in 1886, she bought a two-story, eight-room house on forty-five acres and named it Llanada Villa. By the time she died in 1922, the humble Queen Anne farmhouse had evolved to a 24,000-square-foot sprawling mansion with seven floors, 10,000 windows, 2,000 doors, 160 rooms, fifty-two skylights, forty-seven stairways, seventeen chimneys, thirteen bathrooms, and six kitchens. Along with the sheer vastness, there are strange aberrations that baffled outsiders: one staircase ends at a ceiling, and another has steps so tiny it takes seven flights to go up one floor. There is one door that opens to thin air, and another door in the floor. It feels chaotic, unrestrained, and irrational, so we assume the woman who built it must be chaotic, unrestrained, irrational, right?

Sarah Lockwood Pardee Winchester was the widow of William Winchester, heir to the Winchester Repeating Arms Company, makers of "the gun that won the West." The legend that has come to dominate her story is that Sarah was guided by angry spirits murdered by the gun that made her rich. She was said to hold nightly séances in a special room with one way in and three ways out and a door that opened to an eight-foot drop to the kitchen below. Other tales claim that the house was designed to confuse the vengeful spirits that tormented her. In one version of the tale, the ghosts told her she would die the moment she stopped building. It was said construction never stopped, that the hammering and sawing went on twenty-four hours a day, every day, for thirty-eight years until her death. But the truth isn't nearly as sensational, and it's more entertaining (and lucrative) to imagine her haunted by guilt and ghosts than concede the house is simply the project of a very wealthy woman with a propensity for architecture.

She might have dabbled in séances, since they were extremely popular then — this was a heyday of the Spiritualist movement after all. War and tuberculosis killed off so many too soon, so it's no wonder that people sought some kind of solace in the hope that their loved ones were still with them in spirit. There's simply no evidence that Sarah did, but I wouldn't blame her. In 1866, William and Sarah's only child, Anne, lived only five and a half weeks before succumbing to marasmus. The couple shared a love of architecture, and their way of dealing with their grief was to plunge themselves into the renovation of their house in New Haven. Sarah reveled in every aspect of the project: the design, construction, and planning. Then, in a short ten-month span, her mother died, her father-in-law died, and then tuberculosis took her husband. That tragic spring of 1888 left her bereft but extremely wealthy, and like so many others, she left the East Coast and moved to California to heal and to build. She and her husband processed the death of their daughter in wood and brick, so if séances didn't provide comfort in her mourning, construction certainly did.[14]

She initially hired professional architects, but in the end she preferred to do it herself. Completely self-taught, she studied building manuals, architectural journals, and drafting plans. Rather than a mad woman driven to build by vengeful spirits, the house seems more like a three-dimensional sketchbook of ideas, concepts, and experiments. She called it her "hobby house," and if she didn't like something, she'd scrap it and start over. Her ongoing project also kept her loyal construction crew (whom she paid three times the normal rate) employed in economically tenuous times, which is perhaps where the myth of perpetual construction came from.

The house is Queen Anne style multiplied by a thousand: numerous irregular rooflines with spires and iron cresting, cross gables, and turret after turret after turret. There are elaborate ornamental embellishments and textures with fish-scale shingles on the exteriors and embossed wallcoverings on the inside. But it's the oddities that are the selling point, the strange details assigned supernatural inspiration. They all have reasonable explanations: pillars and columns were installed upside down, not out of some superstitious belief that it was good luck, but because it was more structurally sound. Frank

Lloyd Wright would do the same with his "lily pad" columns in the SC Johnson company building almost fifty years later. The odd corral of tiny switchback steps was not to disorient the spirits but rather her solution for managing her crippling arthritis. A pioneer in accessible design, their size simply made it easier for her to climb the steps. The occasional random windows in the floor were simply lightwells, interior windows to bring additional light to the lower floors.

The great earthquake of 1906 took its toll on the house, but instead of rebuilding like a proper citizen, she sealed the damaged areas off, resulting in stairways to ceilings and doors opening to the air where there was once a balcony. But she was ridiculed for not restoring the house to its previous state. The general desire of those responsible for the architectural character of the city was to encourage rebuilding, to return the city to what it was. Her refusal to comply was considered an act of antisocial rebellion.

Her unwillingness to play her part as the wealthy widow stoked the rumors of her madness. She often declined invitations and avoided her neighbors. Some believed that her unwillingness to finish the house came from a desire to avoid guests. I can identify. She was extremely private and never talked to the press, so if she wouldn't give them a story, they'd make one up for her. The press and the public decided she was a superstitious, misanthropic, obsessive recluse wracked with guilt for profiting off the scores of dead from the Winchester rifles, and perhaps worst of all, she was childless. But she never responded to the rumors and allegations. Neither confirming nor denying, she did something unfathomable: she chose not to participate. Sarah's house was also a witch house.

Only six months after her death in 1922, the house was

sold to John and Mayme Brown, who originally intended to turn it into an amusement park. Public curiosity about the "spook palace" outweighed the desire for a rollercoaster, so it opened for tours as Winchester Park. It was none other than Harry Houdini who, after a visit, dubbed it "the Mystery House."

The "Winchester Mystery House" is probably the least haunted "haunted" house in the United States, but its fabricated mythology persists. Over twelve million people have wandered Sarah's house since it was opened to the public in 1923; touted as the "house that spirits built," it's a must-see destination for the ghost-hunting reality shows. In an episode of *Ghost Adventurers*, host Zak Bagans implies something sinister or malevolent in the house's many hallways and doors. He states with theatrical confidence that the house was constructed with "sacred geometry," that the unusual angles were "meant to connect with the astral plane of the spirits of victims who died by her family's rifles." Zac and his team of ghost bros confrontationally point rifles into the camera, threatening ghosts to speak on cue. It is the ease with which these men speak for her that angers me. They assign motivations to her for entertainment value and give the ghosts credit for her work. On the other hand, it will always be entertaining for me to see grown men scream and jump in terror at the slightest breeze. If Sarah was there, haunting her own home, I hope she scared the piss out of them. In an outtake, after complaining to a museum employee about how confusing it is to find the bathroom, the exasperated young woman says to Zac, "It took me two days to learn the house. It's not that hard!"

In *Winchester* (2018), Sarah (Helen Mirren) sits in her séance room, as spirits guide her hand like a human drafting machine, sketching floorplans of the rooms where they died. It's a nifty twist to the legend, a novel explanation for the seemingly random construction. She hands these spectral working drawings over to her crew, the room is built, and the door boarded shut with thirteen nails, locking the ghosts inside forever. She is depicted as an extremely intelligent, quick-witted, serious, sensitive, and rational woman on the board of the Winchester Repeating Arms Company. But she's still taking orders from ghosts.

The approach to the house is unexpectedly banal. It's on a rather generic commercial street across from a senior-living apartment complex, and from the outside there's no sense of the expanse beyond its front doors. It looks like a grand house for sure, but there's nothing particularly unusual about it, and at only three stories, it feels a bit small compared to the office buildings around it. But in the foyer is a large, framed photo, a bird's-eye view of the property that offers a more authentic perspective. It is a chaotic mix of overlapping gables, rising and falling at different levels, an almost organic forest of red shingles with a comically simplistic arrow marking "You Are Here." Its unpredictability is unnerving; there's a labyrinthian quality, and the seemingly random placement of windows, doors, and rooms is surreal. I understand the desire to assign it more mystical attributes, but the house is only mysterious because we don't live there. It's not meant for us. Sarah did what she wanted to do in the way she wanted to do it, with her own money, but the ghost story takes away her agency and the brilliance of her ingenuity. Her domestic innovations are from the unique perspective of a woman, inventing methods for making housework easier for her staff. Her patented porcelain laundry tubs were molded with built-in washboards and soap holders, and the curved edges in the corners of the steps made sweeping easier. Hers was one of the 1 percent of homes in the U.S. at the time with an indoor heated shower, and while the jets seem a bit too low, it was so the spray wouldn't get her very expensive hairdo wet.[15] She built her house in a time when wealthy women were expected to decorate their homes, not build them. At a time when it was expected for her to open her house to society, invite callers, and host parties, she kept her house to herself. Rather than marketing the house as an extraordinary example of self-taught architecture from before women had the right to vote, the credit is given to the ghosts. Ancient Egyptians couldn't possibly have built the Pyramids of Giza. Must have been aliens. A woman couldn't have conceived of a house like this on her own. She must have been insane.

Like Ted Kaczynski and Ed Gein (and his fictional protégés), Sarah Winchester's legacy is inextricably linked to the character of her house. But unlike the others, Sarah's house is not a sign of psychopathy, rage, or madness, but of curiosity, innovation, play, and unabashed individuality. Even if the real Sarah Winchester did hold séances, it doesn't diminish her accomplishments. As someone sympathetic to the paranormal, I think you can be completely reasonable and intelligent and still think there might be ways of connecting to the other side. But those who knew Sarah insisted that she didn't. "Resentment lies in the heart of the faithful few who served their eccentric mistress against the common gossip which they choose to call infamous lies."[16] Her "faithful servants and the infinitesimal handful of friends" described her as perfectly sane, incredibly intelligent, and "tender-hearted." When she passed away on 5 September, 1922, at the age of eighty-five, Henrietta Sivera, her nurse, secretary, and companion, was with her. As the informant for the official death record, when asked to declare Sarah Winchester's occupation, Henrietta answered rather cheekily, "housewife."[17]

Little Houses

Domestic Doppelgangers

"The doll house erases all but *the frontal view*; its appearance is the realization of the self as property, the body as container of objects, perpetual and incontaminable."

— Susan Stewart, *On Longing*

The poster shows the façade of a very well-known Dutch Colonial with a pair of glowing quarter-arch windows, with a little girl with long blond hair in a white nightgown sitting facing the house in a clear homage to *Poltergeist*. In Steven White's direct-to-video *Amityville Dollhouse* (1996), newlywed couple Bill and Claire Martin move their family into a new house designed and built on the site where a deranged father set fire to the previous house, killing his family.

Bill finds an old dollhouse (the spitting image of the *Amityville* house) in a shed and gives it to his daughter Jessica for her birthday. The presence of the dollhouse affects everyone in the family in all sorts of ways: the little girl immediately starts feeling ill; Bill's stepson Jimmy starts getting visits from his zombified dead father; Claire starts getting overcome with horniness for her teenage stepson Todd; Bill is tormented by nightmares of his daughter dying in a fire. Avoiding any kind of copyright infringement, any similarity to the original movie ends with the design of the dollhouse.[1]

Dollhouses often appear in horror as a shorthand for creepiness. The doll, a humanoid, inanimate object made temporarily alive through play, seems "on the verge of agency," [2] with solid glass eyes that might actually see, little articulated limbs that may actually move, and prerecorded messages turned sentient. They are by their very nature susceptible to human possession, and their residence in the uncanny valley is the dollhouse.

The dollhouse, as a representation of both childhood innocence and the comfort of home, is a perfect target for corruption. The dollhouse is a reminder of a time when we were the most vulnerable, when we had the least power or control over our lives, and when the world still had some magic and mystery. It serves as a symbol for a myriad of fears: of being trapped, manipulated, under surveillance, infantilized, or objectified. If our houses are a reflection of ourselves, dollhouses are miniature replicants of the psyche. They can mimic our reality or serve as projections of our desires. In horror, they can portend disaster, reveal crimes, or be sentient actors with their own agenda, either for good or evil. They can be clairvoyant, all-knowing entities able to portray events from the past, the present, and even the future. They can be the material containers for our shadow selves, housing the darker hidden aspects of our consciousness. They can be doppelgangers mimicking whatever diabolical deeds we may have committed in the real world. If the purpose of the dollhouse is to reenact ordinary life, they can be the perfect instrument with which to pervert the stability of the home by proxy.

Dining room of an antique doll's house, Custom Life Science Images;
and *Barbie's Dreamhouse*, 1962, Stephen Chung.

Dollhouses didn't start as toys the way we think of them now — as imaginative tools for play, with which children (usually girls) can practice domesticity — but as a way for wealthy women to flaunt the objects of their affluence. The dollhouse has its origins in seventeenth-century Germany and Holland, serving as miniature inventories of furniture, books, and art in extravagant homes. They were exquisitely made objects, incredibly expensive to make, and were focused on showcasing the domestic space. After World War I, Queen Mary commissioned a dollhouse to show off the best of British products. Fifteen hundred craftsmen were enlisted to make hundreds of objects: a tiny clock by Cartier; tiny guns by James Purdy & Sons; a fully functional, scaled-down wind-up gramophone by HMV; tiny containers of Colman's mustard; Gilbey's gin; and a little Rolls-Royce Silver Ghost with a silver-tipped whiskey flask in the door.

The dollhouse didn't become popular as a toy for children until the nineteenth century, when changing attitudes about child-rearing put emphasis on childhood and play. The classic style of dollhouse has the façade of a two-story Victorian,

Georgian, or Second Empire, the princess dress of houses. The other side opens to reveal a cross section of spaces to fill with little things representing big things and little people representing big people.

When Barbie, in all her singlehood, got a place of her own in 1962, it was a mid-century modern studio apartment with a built-in bookcase, a loveseat, a coffee table, a tv console, a recliner in the corner, and a painfully small closet. For a dreamhouse, it was pretty attainable. She would eventually graduate from an apartment to a house, and when Barbie got famous, her houses got bigger. Now they include such dreamy amenities as a working elevator, a party room with a DJ booth, a second-story slide with a pool, a balcony with a repositionable hammock swing, and a puppy play area with its own pool and slide. (Yes, even the puppies have their own slide and pool.) It's a child's image of a dream life in an idealized home for a young woman with an idealized body.

Todd Haynes' 1987 short film *Superstar: The Karen Carpenter Story* begins in black and white, with a first-person perspective of someone walking into a home (a real one). We accompany them past the kitchen and living room, and into the bedroom, where we get a glimpse of an exposed bare leg under a blanket (I'm unsure if it's a real leg or not). *Superstar* uses Barbie dolls to tell the story of Karen Carpenter's career and her losing battle with anorexia, a commentary on the commodification and policing of women's bodies and the emotional price of fame. The characters have the stiff, wobbly movement of a doll held by the legs, like a child at play. Recreated in miniature are her parents' house, where she was under the weight of her controlling mother, her first apartment (along with tiny Ex-

Lax boxes and ipecac bottles), and finally a hospital room. Using one famous icon to tell the story of another is even more disturbing if you think of it as play; that of a little girl re-enacting the world as she sees it with dolls.

Dollhouses are a way to imagine other worlds or to cope with the one we are in. As Simon Garfield says, "We bring things down to size to understand and appreciate them. Something too big to visualize at full scale may be rendered comprehensible at 1:12."[3] Those things can be emotions, fears, or demons, figurative or otherwise. Because of the many ways they can represent human states of being, the dollhouse as body/self has become a common contrivance, for better or worse.

Children are gods when they're at play, and the dollhouse is their domain, where the child can create their own world, through the framework of domesticity, a world exactly the way they want, with people behaving exactly the way they want them to. Inside those ¼-inch thin wood walls, they are the ones in charge. Or they are supposed to be. Garfield writes that "the toys we enjoy as children invest us with a rare power at a young age, conferring the potency of adults, and possibly giants. We may never have such dominion over the world again."

In the 2019 *Creepshow* episode "The House of the Head," little Evie (Cailey Fleming) has a gorgeous, beautifully outfitted dollhouse for a small doll family of three she's named the Smith Smiths. Before she goes to school, she lays Mr and Mrs Smith Smith down on their bed and sits their little boy, who she's named Ethan, on the couch in the den to watch tv. But when she comes home, she finds a grotesque severed head on the living room coffee table. She says, "Who are you? What are you doing there? I didn't put you there." The Smith

Smiths are not where she left them. Mom and dad are now sitting up with frozen expressions of worry, and downstairs, Ethan is huddled in the corner in fear. Every time she leaves or turns away, she comes back to find the scene in her dollhouse changed, with the Smith Smiths in a little more peril and the head in a different place in the house. "Smith Smiths," she says, "I think you're haunted." Evie tries to get a handle on things, it's her house after all. She tells them not to move and commanding the Head to leave the Smith Smiths alone.

Meanwhile, in her real world, in her real house, Evie's parents have no idea what's going on in their daughter's room. At one point the Smith Smiths have resorted to prayer, so Evie does the same, asking her befuddled parents if they could say grace before dinner. She decides the Smith Smiths need more help than she alone can provide, so after a trip to the toy store, she returns with a tiny police officer. To no one's surprise, this doesn't help. She goes back to the toy store and asks for a priest or a rabbi. They don't have any tiny religious figures, but they do have a Native American figure, and according to the clerk at the store, "They're very spiritual people." But he doesn't fare any better than the cop. Evie ends up doing the only thing she can. She tells her parents she doesn't want the dollhouse anymore, and at a yard sale they unload it onto some other little girl to deal with.

It's a form of betrayal when the dollhouse breaks the chain of authority. In the big house, the real house, adults are in charge, they make the rules, they craft the world they choose for their child. The dollhouse allows the child to reimagine the home in their own image, designing domestic spaces and familial relationships as they see fit, to play with having power. The dollhouse offers a deconstruction of the world they were given made into something new, the world as they think it should be. As a home inside of a home, the dollhouse contains wishes, dreams, and hopes, like a three-dimensional diary. In *On Longing*, Susan Stewart writes, "Occupying a space within an enclosed space, the dollhouse's aptest analogy is the locket or the secret recesses of the heart: center within center, within within within. The dollhouse is a materialized secret." Dollhouses are intimate, personal, private spaces. Safe spaces to enact fantasies, vent frustrations, and face fears. One of the most fundamental qualities of the home is its sense of privacy; home is where we have the ability to control who enters and who is excluded, who has access and who does not. In a haunting, that power is stolen, and a dollhouse is no different.

Shadow Boxes

"What do you do when the haunted house… is you?"

— Lauren P. Banks, "A Southern Gothic Dollhouse"

"Look at the doll's house! If you look at the house, you'll remember!" It's England, just after the Great War, and Florence Cathcart is doing her best to avoid a dollhouse replica of her childhood home. On the other side of its hinged façade is a miniature re-enactment of her past: her doll self as a child standing in between her doll mother, lying bleeding to death from a gunshot to the stomach, and her doll father, pointing a rifle to his tiny daughter's head. The little boy urging her on is Tom, the ghost of her stepbrother, the second victim of her father's murderous rage, and he's grown impatient, waiting for her to face the trauma she's successfully repressed for years.

In *The Awakening* (2011), Florence (Rebecca Hall), a professional paranormal de-bunker, is summoned to a boarding school to investigate a haunting suspected to be the ghost of a little boy murdered years ago when the building was a private home. It takes her a while to remember that the home was hers, but Tom's use of the dollhouse as a trigger was just the thing to unearth repressed traumatic experiences.

When she first discovers the dollhouse it's empty, just an old toy abandoned in a storage room. But the dollhouse moves around, strategically putting itself in her path so she'll find it, and the next time she sees it, the rooms have been furnished, each set up like little a diorama depicting the events that have occurred since her arrival: her meeting the headmaster, whose arms were overloaded with a stack of books; a student stands with his arm outstretched and palm up waiting for the teacher's cane; she sees herself in another room setting up her ghost-detecting devices; and herself kneeling in front of a hole in the wall, spying on the handsome but shell-shocked teacher while he bathes. The dollhouse has been keeping track of her every movement, moment by moment, since she got there, including her miniature twin, bent over and looking into a tiny replica of the dollhouse she's in front of, just as she is at that moment. However, in the dollhouse version, the figure of a little boy is behind her. When she turns around to an empty room, there's no little boy there, just the door swinging gently. The final time she sees the house, she's confronted with the past her mind firmly shut out, her faceless, murdered little family rendered in felt. The dollhouse is an omniscient entity that knows what's happening in every room at every moment. It sees the past and the present at once, like a ghost, and it remembers what we'd like to forget.

When I was little, I had an imaginary friend named Jack. I also had an imaginary eagle that was the size of our backyard, but he wasn't around a lot since he was always at "eagle camp." Jack was bad. He was so bad he stole police cars, which I imagined in my child mind as the ultimate crime. If something bad was going down in my world, it was probably Jack's fault.

In *Daniel Isn't Real* (2019), Luke (Miles Robbins) also has a very bad imaginary friend, who after decades of imprisonment in a dollhouse is finally set free to do the bad things his real-life friend doesn't have the guts to do.

As a small boy, Luke witnesses a horrific mass shooting, and as a coping mechanism immediately conjures an imaginary friend named Daniel (Patrick Schwarzenegger). Daniel is taller, older, cooler, and has slicked-back hair that makes him look like a greaser from the '50s. Daniel's got it all under control. In the beginning, play with his "imaginary friend" is sweet and normal: they sword fight as knights; Daniel teaches Luke how to make an origami tea set for his mom. He also convinces Luke to dump all his mother's antipsychotic meds into a smoothie because it would give her "magic powers."

Surviving her son's murder attempt, she tells Luke to symbolically lock Daniel up in his grandmother's dollhouse, which he does reluctantly, leaving his friend miniaturized and furious, trapped in a little glowing red room forever. His mother covers the dollhouse with a blanket and then that's that. No more trauma! Fast-forward to college and Luke is all grown-up but having panic attacks and hallucinations triggered by one of his mother's psychotic episodes. On his therapist's advice, he opens the dollhouse, releasing Daniel. Symbolically, of course. His grown-up alternate identity is back, and smarmy as ever, to help Luke adapt. He boosts his self-confidence, hypes him up, and helps him pick up girls. With Daniel free, Luke is more spontaneous and fun, less socially awkward and introverted. But as Daniel takes over more and more of Luke's identity, his behavior gets more chaotic, more dangerous, and more violent. And this time Luke is the one who ends up trapped in the dollhouse.

It's not a subtle metaphor. The dollhouse serves as a physical Jungian space where Luke's shadow self can stay securely shoved down and stored away. The dollhouse, locked up and covered with a blanket, keeps all that repressed trauma contained and hidden, out of sight, out of mind. In Ari Aster's *Hereditary* (2018), miniaturist Annie Graham (Toni Collette) does the exact opposite. She does not lock her pain away inside of a box and throw a blanket over it. She uses the house/dollhouse to exteriorize her pain in balsa wood and paint, giving form to her most painful memories in minute detail. Her miniatures are not toys, and they are not to be played with (dollhouses are toys for kids, miniatures are art for adults). They function as three-dimensional journal entries, and Annie processes her trauma by recreating it at a manageable size. When she sees the ghost of her mother in the corner of her workroom, she does what a lot of us would do: she goes online. Her laptop is open to a site with an article called "Norms on Discerning Presumed Apparitions: Methods of Communication," but as the camera pans, we see she's doing what she does to process the experience. She's painting, in the tiniest of detail, a reproduction of the screen on a tiny laptop. She quite literally compartmentalizes her sorrow, fear, and anger, as it happens, with clinical distance. Through the course of the movie, Annie has been preparing for a gallery exhibition of her work, and in one humorous moment, we see her planning out the exhibition with a miniature model of the gallery, inside of which is a miniature of the gallery model she's working on, a *mise en abyme*[4] of her anxiety.

In the opening shot, we're inside the house, looking out of the window at another form of miniature, a treehouse. A treehouse is a middle step between a dollhouse and an actual house, a transitional space in between play and reality. As the camera zooms out and pans across Annie's work room, we see her history in dioramas: the bedroom where Annie's father starved himself to death and where her brother hung himself is called *The Keep Out Room*. There's *Charlie's Preschool*, the room of her daughter's special-needs class, and *The Hospice* where her mother lays dying in a hospital bed. Finally, we see the replica of the family house and the present day. Focused on her son Peter's (Alex Wolff) miniature bedroom, the camera gets closer until we lose the edge of the dollhouse as a frame. When the door opens, Peter's father moves into the room and we are seamlessly transitioned into the real world, setting us up immediately to question if anything happening to this family is under their control, or if they are all being played with.

Hereditary (2018), Ari Aster

When her daughter, Charlie (Milly Shapiro), is killed in a horrific accident, Annie does what she does and makes a miniature of the event. She faithfully crafts the telephone pole her speeding son swerved a little too close to while trying to avoid roadkill. There's Charlie's arm hanging out of the family station wagon when, in allergy-induced anaphylactic shock, she leaned out of the window desperate for air. When her husband sees Annie carefully painting a trail of blood on the road leading from her daughter's miniature decapitated head, he is understandably angry and disgusted. But she's emotionally detached, saying with passive-aggressive confusion, "What? It's a neutral view of the accident." This is what the process of miniaturization does: it takes the unbearable and neutralizes it. Annie took her all-consuming despair and made it manageable and safely pocket sized.

Throughout the film, scenes are framed in impossibly wide shots (the whole interior of the house was built on a set with moveable walls), so the family is dwarfed in their own space. This is perhaps why the sets have a minimal perfection that feels unnatural. Are they enlarged versions of miniatures or miniature versions of a real place? There are no reflections in Annie's bedroom mirrors, they're just flat metallic surfaces, like a dollhouse mirror. In a bird's-eye view, the house is barely visible in the trees, dwarfed in the landscape. The house was never truly a home, since home implies agency, comfort, trust, and safety, the things Annie's mother never provided. Just as a dollhouse can never be a home, neither can the Graham family house.

One of the more extraordinary miniatures gets very little screen time. Tucked near the stairs in the foyer is the "Quicksand House." A house rests on top of a grassy surface and just below is another house suspended in the dirt and rocks, dingy and decayed. At the bottom of the form is an even older house, twisted and disintegrating. Each house is a different generation of Annie's family represented by a different architectural style: the modern house above ground is Peter, the Colonial buried just below is Annie, and the Victorian at the very bottom is her mother. The sculpture is a cross section of trauma on top of trauma, an immaculately constructed return of the repressed in 1:12 scale.

Tiny Crimes

"I have been working on the bodies and have three of them done, dressed, posed, and quite definitely dead."

— Frances Glessner Lee

Adora Crellin is the wealthy apex social predator of Wind Gap, Missouri, and her house is perfect. The robin's-egg blue-green Queen Anne with the grey shingled roof, white trim, and a wraparound veranda is perfect for gossiping with the ladies and day-drinking spiked sweet tea. Her house is *Architectural Digest*–ready at any given moment, as is she. The De Gournay wallpaper is hand-painted from Paris. There's no air-conditioning, despite the brutal heat, because Adora finds window units "tacky." Rooms are painted "Arsenic green," alluding to a time when green pigment was poison, and nodding to Adora's Munchausen-by-proxy form of maternal care.[5] But the showstopper of Adora's house is her bedroom floor tiled with ivory. It is a beautiful but grotesque artifact: slices of elephant, rhinoceros, walrus, and whale tusks, made back when it was still legal. It is a delicate, pristine display of wealth made from cruelty. Just like Adora.

In the HBO series *Sharp Objects* (2018), based on the book

by Gillian Flynn, Adora's (Patricia Clarkson) eldest daughter, Camille (Amy Adams), is a reporter returning home to cover the murder of two teenage girls. The girls, about the same age as her stepsister, Amma (Eliza Scanlen), were strangled to death, with one unusual detail: all their teeth had been pulled out. To her mother's constant embarrassment and disappointment, Camille is not perfect. Very far from it. Unlike the pastel dresses of her mother, the knit twinsets of her old schoolmates, and the flowing caftans of her mother's best friend, her wardrobe consists entirely of black jeans and grey long-sleeve T-shirts to hide her scars. Her skin is a word cloud of self-harm, a private method of constructed control.

Adora's vice-like grip on propriety extends past the house and on to her children. Her thirteen-year-old daughter Amma's bedroom is full of aggressively girly saturated pinks and tufted furniture. At home, she dresses for her mother in prim and proper floral dresses with a bow in her hair like a doll. But outside the house, Amma rules her gang of mean girls in cut-offs, roller skating through town on ecstasy. She plays the part of the sweet, yet often mysteriously ill, daughter with sociopathic accuracy.

Amma's dominion is her dollhouse, an exact replica of Adora's house, and she exerts just as much exacting control over it. If her mother changes the upholstery of a chair, Amma must have the same pattern for its miniature. Everything must be perfect. She tells Camille that the dollhouse is her "fancy." It's an oddly old-fashioned word for a teenager, a word Adora would use, suggesting her delight in manipulating the miniatures in the dollhouse and the people in the real house.

If children are gods at play, Amma chooses to be Persephone, Queen of the Underworld, and her miniature interpretation of her mother's ivory floor takes it one step further. Instead of animal tusks, Amma tiles her mother's tiny bedroom with the teeth of the girls she's murdered: "Fifty-six tiny teeth, cleaned and bleached and shining from the floor."[6] In the book, she doesn't stop with teeth. For Camille's room, she makes a rug woven with the hair of one of her victims. One has to appreciate the craftmanship. The dollhouse is indeed perfect.

The use of dollhouses to reveal crimes is a well-worn device, but *The Dollhouse Murders* — a made-for-tv movie from 1992 — might be one of my favorites. A low-fidelity version is available on YouTube, but the sound occasionally falls out. Fortunately, it doesn't really impede your understanding of the movie. While staying with her Aunt Clare (Lindsay Jackson), teenager Amy (Amanda Rowse) finds a dollhouse replica of her aunt's house. When she finds the miniature figures of her extended family, Amy and her friend Ellen (Hillary Brooks) set them up around the dining room, but Aunt Clare tells her ominously that the girl doll should be positioned upstairs after being sent up to her room for "impertinence." But the dolls refuse to stay where they are put. When Amy returns to the attic the next day, the grandfather is on the floor next to the bed, the grandmother is toppled over in the dining room, and Clare's little brother is hiding in the closet. Unlike for Evie in "The House of the Head," this soon escalates to her witnessing the dolls move right in front of her eyes. After the requisite research trip to the library, Amy discovers that her great-grandparents and her uncle were murdered, and the dolls keep returning again and again to the positions in which they died. Each time the house lights up and comes to life, they know they are getting closer and closer to the moment of truth. "It's starting!" Amy cries, like she's watching a play.

The great-grandma doll in the parlor moves closer and closer, pointing to the miniature bookcase, her little face frozen in terror. Amy cries out, "I don't want to see the murder!" covers her eyes and runs away. The girls, taking their cue from the great-great-grandmother doll, search through the parlor bookcase until they find a letter folded inside a copy of Ibsen's *A Doll's House* declaring the handyman the murderer. Mystery solved. The clues were in the dollhouse the whole time, they just needed to keep looking.

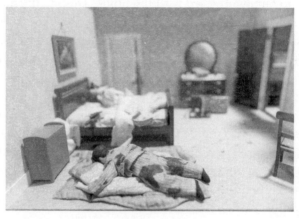

Case in the *Nutshell Studies*, model of "An Unexplained Double Murder," Edwin Remsberg

Susan Stewart says that "the miniature is the notation of the moment and the moment's consequences," and no one understood that like Frances Glessner Lee. She understood how freezing a moment in a tableau allows for a close examination of a life, creating time for inspection and discovery, and how the simple act of taking something mundane and shrinking it down can make it extraordinary. *The Nutshell Studies of Unexplained Death* is not a movie or a film, but a collection of dollhouses (or dioramas, if we want to be professional about it) depicting the deaths of ordinary people in ordinary homes. They are little morbid crime scenes created not for show or for play, but to train law enforcement to be better at their job. Lee believed that "the investigator must bear in mind that he has a twofold responsibility — to clear the innocent as well as to expose the guilty. He is seeking only the facts — the truth in a nutshell."

Frances Glessner Lee was born in 1878 into a wealthy Chicago family obsessed with the home. Despite the massive, fortress-like stone exterior, the interior of the Glessner's Arts and Crafts mansion on Prairie Avenue reflected their desire for a simpler, cozier, and warmer home than the typical Gilded Age mansion. Built right up to the edge of the property, with no front yard and few windows, it resembles a jail more than a home, but the focus of the house was directed inward, toward a large and open courtyard. Frances' father, John Glessner, wrote a book glorifying the home called *The Story of a House*, and her mother kept meticulous records of household activities. The *Nutshell* dollhouses are also focused on the interiors and the activities that happen inside, "a continuation or perversion of her parent's obsession with their home."[7]

Frances lived the sheltered and privileged life of the rich, one that was dominated by the idealized "feminine household." Despite her longing for an education, her parents forbade her to go to college, so she did what she was expected to do: she married an incompatible but socially appropriate man when she was nineteen and had three children. She and her husband would eventually divorce, and her son attributed the failed marriage partly to her "creative urge coupled with the desire to make things."[8] Her life had been dictated by interiors, by a one-sided perspective of what the life of a woman should be, so it's logically satisfying that she would turn this feminine art of crafting into a career in what (at the time) was an entirely male field. In her later years, instead of sitting back into the predictable role of a society matron, Lee spent her leisure time creating miniature dioramas of grisly crime scenes and would become known as the mother of forensic science.

Around 1930, she met a friend of her brother's, George Burgess Magrath, and this would change the course of her life. He was professor in pathology at Harvard and the chief medical examiner of Suffolk County. She did what I would do: corner this guy at a dinner party and ask him all the grisly details of his job. They would talk about his work and the bungled cases due to officers losing and mishandling evidence. She was fascinated by criminology and the theory that scientific analysis of material evidence was the key to solving crimes. She created *The Nutshell Studies of Unexplained Death* as a training tool with which to teach investigators how to more carefully examine crime scenes. The point wasn't to try to solve the crime, but to train detectives to look at crime scenes differently, more carefully, to see all the minute details in a scene, details that could be easily overlooked, and to hone their skills of observation. The goal was not just to note the obvious, but for the detectives to work their way through the scene, slowly and methodically, to get the whole picture, to (as she put it) "look at the scene at the effective moment, very much as if a motion picture were stopped at such a point. The inspector may best examine them by imagining himself as a trifle less than six inches tall."

Even though she was born and raised in wealth, she was deeply concerned with issues of the underprivileged and the marginalized, and her scenes usually took place in ordinary working-class homes: tenements, boarding houses, barns, and farmhouses, and most of the victims, as in real life, were women in domestic spaces. Each had a story attached to them, composites of real cases adding details to their lives. For example, the model *Dark Bathroom* shows a scene as discovered by a woman called Lizzie Miller:

> *I roomed in the same house as Maggie, but we only spoke when we met in the hall. I think she was subject to fits (seizures). A couple of male friends came to see her fairly regularly. Tonight, the men were in her room, and there seemed to be a good deal of drinking going on. Sometime after they left, I heard the water still running in the bathroom, so I opened the door and found Maggie dead in the tub with water pouring down her face.*

It's a bathroom with dark, paneled wood walls and yellow patterned wallpaper. There is a line of laundry hanging from the ceiling with a few items held in place with meticulously crafted clothes pins. Pinned to the wall next to the toilet is a batch of white slips of cloth. Then you see the legs draped over the edge of the tub; the oversize knit texture of black stockings (Lee knit the stockings with needles the size of straight pins); the white lace bloomers under a blue-and-white striped skirt with red trimmed hem. Upon closer inspection, we see the rest. The doll is lying face up in the tub, reddish-brown hair surrounding a white porcelain face with painted eyes wide open as a pillar of white resembling a stream of water pours over her frozen mouth. The little chain for the bathtub plug hangs over the side, and on the edge is a little bar of brownish-yellow soap in a white dish and a medicinal-looking bottle with stains of liquid dripping down the side. On the floor are two different patterned rugs overlapping each other… this is just the beginning. The more you look, the more you see, which is exactly the point. In this one snapshot of a room are a million little details of a life and death.

It's a horrifying scene, made even more disturbing as it's depicted in the visual language of play, but it's hard not to be charmed by the attention to detail, by the exquisite craft. Lee was serious about her work, but she must have delighted in the making given the unwavering commitment to accuracy and the precision of the production, not only of the houses, but of the victims as well, "carefully sticking a knife into a lower abdomen or painting a face the crimson pink of carbon monoxide poisoning."[9]

One dollhouse would take about three months to complete, which seems fast to me considering the depth of detail, which involved choosing just the right kind of fabric for the dress of a working-class woman, and picking the correct wallpaper pattern to match the victim's lifestyle. Ashtrays were filled with the butts of real tiny cigarettes; miniature coffeepots contained even more miniature coffee grounds; even the miniature mousetraps worked. In remaking the minutia of a household, she immersed herself in their lives in ways a typical police officer or homicide detective never would.

The audience for these dioramas at the time was made up of adult men, not little girls, and I wonder what it would have been like if it was me examining them with a detective's gaze. Would I instinctively reach to move the doll from under the stream of water out of pure habit? Would my first reaction be to "play," not merely observe?

The dollhouse is a life imagined, a rehearsal mimicking what we know and imagining what we hope will be, a mock-up, a proof of concept for domesticity. They provide simplified versions of adult experiences scaled down to fit into a small bedroom and manipulated with small hands. I used to play "meeting" when I was little. Unable yet to write, I would sit at the dining room table taking "notes" on a yellow legal pad borrowed from my mother, pretending to be a very important businessperson. I'm amazed that there was a time in my life when what is now the most tedious part of my day as an adult was playtime. But I knew meetings were things grown-ups did, and they seemed more interesting than changing diapers on baby dolls. I can understand the desire, when "adulting" gets too hard to reverse the process and go back to child-sized life, to a simpler, more compact life. Hopefully one with fewer meetings.

In the 1963 *Twilight Zone* episode "The Miniature," Charlie Parks (Robert Duvall), a repressed, lonely, socially awkward man has not quite mastered being a grown-up. He lives at home with an overprotective mother who turns down his bed for naps and bring him cocoa, but she wants nothing more than to see her Charlie settle down, get married, and move out. He visits a museum on his lunch break and comes across an exhibit of Victorian home life which includes a dollhouse typical of its time. It's labeled:

> *Nineteenth Century Town House. Model of Boston residence of Mr. and Mrs. Copley Summers. The figure represents their daughter, Alice, and was carved in wood from the original balcony.*

In the dollhouse parlor room, Alice (played by a live actor) is seated at a harpsichord, when suddenly she begins to play. He soon realizes, after asking the security guard how such a mechanical marvel is done, that he is the only one who hears her music and sees her move. He is immediately smitten.

He's fired from his job for not being a team player, for being a square peg that doesn't fit in. He's considered robotic and even inhuman by his co-workers. His boss compares him to a "wind-up toy," a notably prescient comparison. Uninterested in getting a new job, or meeting a real woman, he returns to the museum day after day, watching Alice go about her life: she reads, does needlepoint while her maid dusts; a suspicious gentleman suitor comes to take her out. She has a light breakfast of toast, and he reprimands her for not eating enough. He talks to her and tells her about his life and his mother, unbothered by the fact she can't hear, see, or talk to him. Unable to connect to real women, he sees reciprocation in her silence and believes that the doll is in love with him in return. He sees her as innocent, sweet, and proper, the epitome of Victorian lady-like propriety, unlike the sexually forward women of today. After attempting to "break-in" to the dollhouse to save her from the rakish suitor, he's institutionalized. After therapy, he feigns recovery, and ensures his family that he is all better now. He realizes the woman is just an inanimate object made of wood and is ready to get a job and take his place in the real world. But this is just a ruse. He runs away, back to the museum, leaving his family searching for him in vain while he sits, miniaturized, inside of the dollhouse, on the sofa with the love of his very small life.

For Charlie, the dollhouse is a controlled environment where the universe is simplified to a level he can understand, a world where the lack of complexity is a comfort. For children, toys are tools with which to safely practice adulthood, to act out the workings of the world and figure out who they are and what they want to be. They are also therapeutic devices with which to express the unbearable, to transpose pain onto plastic and cloth and let the doll carry the emotional burden. They are surrogates with which to externalize the internal, and in horror, they provide a device to either express or repress the darkest parts of ourselves.

There is an uncanny blend of malevolence and innocence in a dollhouse. In the miniaturization of terrifying events, the horrible becomes unwillingly cute. The miniature is having a comeback, the return of a Victorian hobby, only not as a display of opulence but as an expression of loving reverence for decay and ruin. The "dirty" dollhouse reduces the dull minutiae of the real world into palm-sized treasures, crafting the messy complexities of real life with exacting precision. The gross and dismal becomes sweet and fascinating when downsized. Brooklyn-based miniaturist Danny Cortez sees "beauty in a rust drip,"[10] turning eyesores into a charming homage to the grit of New York City: a rusted, bent metal garbage can; an old newspaper box layered with graffiti tags and stickers. Ryan Thomas Monahan recreates a worn green door with an "Apartment to Rent" sign, grimy with age, each bit of tiny peeled and scuffed paint immaculately reproduced, an abandoned Blockbuster Video engulfed in weeds.

Lauren P. Banks' *Southern Gothic Dollhouse* is a ghost story told in meticulously crafted miniature objects: a skeleton stuffed inside of a buried toy chest; a door covered in scratch marks and locked shut with old padlocks; a chandelier detailed with baby teeth; occult symbols drawn on the floor of an attic surrounded by a circle of candles and mirrors; jars of honey in a wooden crate on a bed next to a rotting corpse covered in dead flowers. Every room, in perfectly recreated decrepitude, contains the tiny details of an ever-evolving horror story.

It's easy to get lost in the images, rich and layered with precise creepy whimsey, but looking at the pink tiles of a bathroom coated with mildew, a bedroom with a floor layered with dust, and an open wardrobe with moldering gossamer dresses rotting like ghosts, I can imagine how terrifying walking into one of these spaces would be. Reduced and concentrated into the smallest size possible, the things we fear, the things that disgust us, become manageable, controllable, and even adorable when they fit in the palm of your hand.

I had a pretty great dollhouse when I was a kid. It was all wood, a tricked-out kit made to resemble the Tudor house across the street from us in Detroit, which I must have admired at some point (which is funny because I despise Tudor now). We would get kits that I would assemble, painting little model pieces of furniture to supplement the porcelain toilet and bathtub and the brass bed posts. I liked making the furniture more than reenacting domestic scenarios. Over the years, the house moved along with us, packed up in a box folded up to fit it just right. It was big, too big for New York apartments, and I realized at some point I had to let it go. Tossing it out as if it was just a plastic Fisher-Price toy was out of the question. Even donating it to Goodwill felt like abandoning it. I finally gave it to a friend's son as a birthday present, which seemed like a respectful thing to do. He loved it for a while and then outgrew it, as all kids do. Once again, I was left with the question of what to do with this massive remnant of my childhood. I think I wanted it to mean more to me than it did; the care and craft that went into it felt like something too precious to let go of. But when we finally decided to donate it to a women's shelter, that felt right. There are some things I have that mean more, for whatever reason: my first teddy bear, my old copy of *The Little Prince*. The dollhouse didn't have the emotional grip I would have thought it would. Perhaps because it wasn't our house, it didn't look like my home. I'm grateful, because if horror movies have taught me anything, it's to never make a dollhouse replica of your own house. But I did keep the furniture.

Forever Houses

When the shit hits the fan

"It is still 90 seconds to midnight."

> — 2024 Doomsday Clock Statement, Science and
> Security Board, *Bulletin of the Atomic Scientists*

> *Ladybug! Ladybug!*
> *Fly away home.*
> *Your house is on fire.*
> *And your children all gone.*
> *All except one,*
> *And that's little Ann,*
> *For she crept under*
> *The frying pan.*

In the 1963 film *Ladybug, Ladybug,* an elementary school in the Southern California countryside is disrupted by the wailing of an emergency siren. The teachers, fully trained in nuclear war preparedness, aren't sure if it's a real attack or a drill, but with anxious professionalism, they escort the children to their homes, dropping them off one by one to deliver the news of their impending doom to their parents. The particularly authoritative Harriet (Alice Playten) invites her remaining classmates over to her house since she's the one with the bomb shelter. It's safe to say that Harriet is the "little Ann" of the group. With her parents not at home, she assumes responsibility for the children's survival and immediately takes charge of the situation, assigning jobs and making rules. She rations out cups of water, schedules meals of MPF (multi-purpose food), and assures the group that thanks to the air pump her father installed, they have enough air. For now. When they're not busy deciding who lives and who dies, they pass the time by sharing what they want to be when they grow up. One boy wants to be an engineer, another girl just says, "A mother." Harriet wants to be a model because "you get your picture taken and wear new dresses all day." Steve, one of the eldest at twelve, has fully succumbed to existential dread. He looks up with a thousand-yard stare and asks, "Grow…up?", as if the very concept is absurd.

The film is inspired by a real incident that occurred in 1962 at Miraleste Elementary School in Rancho Palos Verdes, California, when at 8:40 am, the school's emergency signal system unexpectedly sounded a "yellow alert." The teachers, assuming it was real, escorted their students out and were on the road before they were told it was a false alarm ten minutes later. But for those ten minutes, a group of children and their teachers thought the end of the world was imminent, that today could be their last day on earth, and all they wanted was to get home.[1]

A year before, the 15 September, 1961, issue of *Life* magazine featured a photo of a man in a "civilian" radiation suit, hand raised to shield his eyes from the inevitable blast, with the headline "How You Can Survive Fallout." The issue published a letter from President John F. Kennedy urging dads across the country to build bomb shelters in their backyards. Secretary of defense Robert S. McNamara wrote, "There is much you can do to protect yourself and in doing so strengthen your nation." During the Cuban Missile Crisis, the Federal Civil Defense

Administration (FCDA) launched a campaign educating men across the country about their patriotic duty to protect their families and stick it to the commies through home improvement.

Popular Science Monthly, March 1951

Just as homeownership was marketed toward a specific American family portrait, so were bomb shelters. The Office of Civil and Defense Mobilization explicitly targeted suburban, white, middle-class families with a working father, a mother at home, and a few kids. If America was going to survive through a nuclear holocaust, they wanted to make sure the ones who made it out alive were the right sort of people. They weren't particularly interested in the survival of renters and city apartment dwellers, (i.e. Black, brown, and poor people). The campaign fortified the patriarchal authority of the father as protector and the American ideal of rugged individualism. While the women canned the food, the men built the bunkers, because you can't depend on the government to take care of you. That's socialist stuff.

The personal fallout shelter was about protecting personal private property and the single-family unit, not the community or anyone else who might need protecting. In *Ladybug, Ladybug*, one of their schoolmates begs to be let inside, but the children refuse, pressing the door closed against the screaming girl. Harriet asks, "What if my parents come home, my grandmother? There's not enough room!"

In *The Twilight Zone* episode "The Shelter," from 1961, a dinner party at the suburban home of Bill Stockton (Larry Gates) is interrupted when a civil defense announcement comes on tv warning of incoming unidentified flying objects. His friends and neighbors used to make fun of Bill's bomb shelter side project, but not anymore. Finding themselves woefully unprepared for the end of the world, they descend upon Bill's house begging to be let inside. With only enough air, space, and provisions for his own family, he refuses to let them in, and the friends he just had cocktails with less than thirty minutes ago descend into hysterics, anger, and nativism against the one slightly darker, vaguely Mediterranean mustachioed guest, the "pushy grabby, semi-American." They're fighting not only over who should be allowed to live, but who is American enough to live. His neighbor Jerry has the newest house on the block, with "all the advantages of modern architecture with everything at their fingertips, all the wonders of modern science," but without the one thing they need: a basement.

The descendants of the Cold War bunker dads are today's preppers, well stocked on supplies and locked and loaded for any number of catastrophic emergencies. Survival isn't just a hobby, it's a lifestyle. In the National Geographic series *Doomsday Preppers* (2012–2014), there is often a smug superiority in those who prep with the absolute confidence of true believers for when "the shit hits the fan" and the marauding hordes of unprepared will be coming to steal your stuff. When the supply-chain-dependent Pollyannas from the city come running for their stockpiles of MREs and ammunition, they'll be ready. In each episode they are graded on how well they have prepared (the scale being how many more months or years of survival they have to look forward to). Every prepper has their own theory of how the world will come to an end, and there are a lot to choose from: a pandemic (been there, done that); a comet colliding with the Earth; a solar flare; an electromagnetic pulse knocking out the grid; nuclear war or a reactor meltdown; the Earth's axis shifting, causing a pole shift. They don't mention alien invasion, but I wouldn't count that out.

10 Cloverfield Lane (2016), Dan Trachtenberg

In *10 Cloverfield Lane* (2016), Howard Stambler (John Goodman) is a prepper who built his bunker long ago, but it has a deceptively lived-in warmth. The homey farmhouse décor looks like what his home would probably be like, or a vacation cabin in the woods. The living area has striped wallpaper, shelves of curios, and vases of what I assume are fake flowers. The place is warmly lit by an assortment of mismatched table lamps, and the furniture is wood, painted in pale greens and blues worn through with time, including an heirloom table (he insists on coasters and place mats). There's a jukebox stocked with oldies but goodies, and a large selection of DVDs, VHS tapes, books, and board games. It looks like a million other rec rooms and finished basements across the country, but the dome shaped ceiling and tell-tale lack of windows are the only indications that this is not a normal house.

When Michelle (Mary Elizabeth Winstead) first meets Howard, she has just woken up on a mattress on the floor, chained to the wall, bleeding from a car crash. Howard tells Michelle that he found her, brought her to his shelter, tended her wounds, and chained her up "for her own protection." After begging him not to kill her, she asks, "What are you going to do to me?" He answers, "I'm going to keep you alive." He tells her that there's been an attack and leaving the shelter is out of the question. He throws around words like "radiation," "Ruskies," and "Martians," a mélange of classic post-Cold War horror movie threats, none of which are more frightening than being a woman alone in a room with a locked metal door and a strange man demanding gratitude. Emmet (John Gallagher Jr), the other member of this consequential family, corroborates his story, claiming to have seen the blast of bright light with his own eyes and, like the unprepared masses, come banging on Howard's door begging for shelter. Michelle is still wary of Howard, but begins to trust Emmet, and the three soon settle into a domestic routine of '80s movies, board games, and Fluffernutter sandwiches.

There are enough clues to suggest Howard might be right about whatever catastrophe is happening above them: a panicked, mutilated survivor demanding to be let in; ominous unidentifiable rumbling sounds from the surface. But there are also clues that he might be lying and keeping her captive: evidence of a missing girl he claims is his daughter; a body-sized barrel of perchloric acid. The bunker begins to feel less like a finished basement turned doomsday shelter and more like a kidnapper's dungeon. The common perception of the prepper as a paranoid, conspiratorial (usually white) man means Howard is already a suspicious figure, and Howard's paternal temperament turns creepy and threatening. The outlandish threat of alien invasion becomes more absurd compared to the plausible and immediate threat of a potential psychopath. Michelle could be trapped in Howard's bunker forever, alive or dead, and the homey-ness of the décor feels sinister instead of comforting.

In designing the bunker, director Dan Trachtenberg imagined Howard building it after the birth of his daughter Megan in the early 1990s but stopping when his family left him, and the space is frozen in time around 2000. The bare cinderblock cell that becomes Michelle's room is painted half grey and half pink because "it was intended to be Megan's room and was never finished." Michelle is trapped in an underground prison of brown plaids and rustic country décor, an unwilling surrogate daughter to either a paranoid conspiracist or a psychopath, and will remain so for an indeterminate amount of time.[2]

Howard's desire to make his bunker a comfortable home, a place for a family to live, implies a disconcerting acceptance of and perhaps pleasure in "the end of the world as we know it," a satisfaction in being able to thrive rather than just survive without sacrificing any of the pre-apocalyptic comforts of home. There is a new breed of luxury bunker that is a far cry from the basic, middle-class 10x10' bomb shelters of the '50s with cinder block walls, rudimentary wooded shelves, and bunk beds with thin mattresses. The expectations of a late-stage capitalist Armageddon require an uninconvenienced doomsday.

In the Black Hills of South Dakota, past the gate with the military-trained armed guards, underneath the grid of rectangular mounds pushing up from the earth like oblong hobbit houses, is a single-family home resembling something between a mid-level hotel business center and a suburban rec room. There are oversized brown leather recliners with cup holders in which to watch movies in the home theater, a faux-rustic wooden coffee table, bedrooms with brown-and-red patterned shiny pillows and duvets, gleaming stainless-steel appliances, and a long dining room table already set for a candlelit dinner. Strings of bare, warm Edison bulbs are strung along the ceiling, and there's motel art on the walls. It has a forced, cozy Pottery-Barn-meets-Walmart vibe that I imagine is intended to be welcoming but which comes across as the opposite. Everything is totally fine and normal. Nothing to worry about. Its generic, wood-paneled blandness is designed to feel "homey," to comfort and soothe, and to allow people to forget whatever nightmare is happening on the other side of the wall. For a space without natural light, they've made the décor decidedly dark and brown. Personally, I'd prefer bare concrete, but that's me.

F-805 is one of 575 concrete-domed military bunkers at Vivos xPoint built by Robert Vicino. In 1980, Vicino was "divinely inspired to build a shelter for 1,000 people, deep underground to protect us from a coming life-extinction event."[3] He doesn't specify where exactly the message came from (God, aliens: who knows, doesn't matter.) It's a responsibility he accepts "with great humility and gratitude," and like a modern-day Noah, he began the project he's been developing for the past forty-plus years to save humanity from impending doom (at least those humans who can afford to spend $150,000 on a ninety-nine-year lease for a second home they will, hopefully, never use). What would now comfortably house a family of four was originally built in 1942 to store bombs, the very thing Vicino and his survivalist forebears were protecting themselves from in the first place. The door on the outside remains as it was: grey steel with its identifying "address" in huge numbers. The door on the inside is regular, shiny, dark wood with a brass doorknob, incongruous next to the concrete exterior. It's an absurd bit of folly that, in its attempt to create a sense of normalcy, makes the distinction between the danger outside and safety inside even more evident. Despite the wood paneling, the windowless, curved walls give away what the bunkers really are: spaces meant to store missiles, not people.

Larry Hall — another prominent figure in luxury apocalyptic real estate development — has solved the problem of windowless living. Like Vivos, his Survival Condo is a remnant from the Cold War. The former missile silo turned apartment complex is two hundred feet underground and built to withstand a direct nuclear strike. Above the seven floors of $2-to-3-million-dollar luxury apartments are a climbing wall, medical clinic, and a mock grocery store where tenants can pretend to shop for prepaid shelf-stable foods. Below is a library, a classroom, a bar, a gym, a movie theater, a pool room designed to look like a beach, and, of course, a shooting range. According to Hall, these details of ersatz normalcy are crucial in order to avoid depression and cabin fever, "even if the world is burning outside."[4] If the world was indeed burning outside, at least you would be able to see it: embedded in the walls are LED screens displaying a high-definition camera feed of the outside, creating the illusion that residents are not underground. Since the world has not ended yet, the current view is of a green field, a blue sky, and a spinning wind turbine; an idyllic sunny day in some undisclosed location in Kansas. Should reality become too monotonous (or depressing if the world becomes a scorched wasteland), owners can pick a different view of their choosing like a desktop image or Zoom background. Just past the nine-foot-thick epoxy-hardened concrete walls could be a lush forest in Oregon, a beach front in the Bahamas, or a Paris street. You could gaze at the Alps or the backyard of your childhood home. One potential buyer from New York requested a view of Central Park, one for each season, and background traffic noise, adding another illusory sensory experience.

Unlike the tangible and specific potential for thermonuclear annihilation during the Cold War, today's threats are any number of shadowy hypotheticals: sociopolitical upheaval, a nonspecific dread of a changing world, an ill-perceived power shift in demographics, a contrived menace threatening one's firm grasp on the world. To quote Robert Vicino, "The world is crazy. Things are happening. Socially, politically, disasters. Things are unraveling. Nobody can deny it any longer."[5] This need to protect oneself from imagined "crazy things," to go to such lengths to prepare for hypotheticals, is alien to me. Author Mark O'Connell speculates that "preppers are not preparing for their fears: they are preparing for their fantasies."[6]

I have zero desire to survive an apocalypse. When the aliens invade, when the poles shift, I'll be the first bitten, drowned, or plunged into a crevice in the earth. Ever since zombies started moving fast, that marked the end of me. I would be swallowed up in a wave of the sprinting dead, blindly grunting for brains like the rest of them, and I have no problem with that. I'm also lacking in some basic survival instincts. When Hurricane Sandy hit New York City, my disaster prep was mostly buying a pair of bright orange rain boots I thought were cute, stocking up on Oreos, and getting cocktails at my neighborhood bar before they closed because it happened to be called Weather Up. But mostly I don't want to "survive." I've seen *The Last of Us*. It looks miserable.

The belief that the world (or the world as we know it) will "end," resulting in a permanent shift in human beings' place in the universe, is certainly not new. In Zoroastrianism, the term for the end times is "Frashokereti," and it is thought of as the *final renovation* of the universe, which I quite like; the idea that the planet is just being freshened up for new tenants, like flipping a house.

The ways in which Armageddon will occur have gotten more secular, and change as technology changes — so do our fears and our response to those fears. Blame shifts depending on which disenfranchised group is chosen as scapegoat. There have been plenty of world-ending events — ask any Native person in the United States — but when the clouds roll in on the ruling class, the potential for eschatological economic growth is palpable. If the idea of the end of the world isn't new, capital investment in its survival certainly *feels* new. Prepping has become an $11-billion industry, and about a third of Americans now identify themselves as preppers. Those numbers have grown exponentially since we elected the first Black president in 2008, and after the election of Donald Trump in 2016, the number of people preparing for disaster doubled.

While prepping used to be the purview of the right-leaning white survivalists, more marginalized groups have joined in. After the Black Lives Matter protests of 2020, there are more Black and brown preppers, and since the uptick of violence and legislation against LGBTQ+ folks, there's been a growth in queer preppers, the difference being that threats against the marginalized and the oppressed are real, and it's the ones fearing the end of the world as *they* know it who have become the violent hordes.

In *10 Cloverfield Lane*, Howard chastises his guests for joking about how long they might be down in the bunker. The sooner they can acclimate to life inside, the easier it will be to sustain themselves. The sooner they can accept the bunker as a home, the easier it will be to withstand it. Part of the sales pitch for any bunker/condo is how long you would be able to survive inside. Six months? Six years? Six decades? How long does it take for a bunker to become home? If you were born in a bunker, would it ever be a shelter to you, or would it only ever be home?

Raised in captivity

"Do you trust the House? I ask Myself. Yes, I answer Myself. You are the Beloved Child of the House. Be comforted. And I am comforted."

— Piranesi, Susanna Clarke

In Susanna Clarke's novel *Piranesi*, the titular character's world is a house — an extraordinary one, to be sure, one made of endless arched hallways lined with classical sculptures, a house with an internal sea that rises and falls, and one he has no memory of entering and no way of leaving. As far as Piranesi knows, the house is all there is in the world, and there are only two people who exist, himself and another figure known as The Other, whom the house occasionally gifts with supplies and new shoes when he needs them. Piranesi is one of only fifteen people who have ever existed in the world. He knows because he's seen the skeletal remains of the ones before him. He spends his days mending fishing nets, recording the tides, and meeting with The Other for some intellectual discourse. But he is an explorer at heart, a traveler determined to see as much of the house/world as he can in his lifetime. So far, he's seen hundreds if not thousands of hallways, including "the Nine-Hundred-and-Sixtieth Hall to the West, the Eight-Hundred-and-Ninetieth Hall to the North and the Seven-Hundred-and-Sixty-Eighth Hall to the South." He's seen the misty Upper Halls in the clouds, the watery Drowned Halls below, and the ruins of the Derelict Halls of the East. But he has yet to find a border to the house. He has "never seen any indication that the World was coming to an End, but only the regular progression of Halls and Passageways into the Far

Distance." Piranesi's house is more than just his home, it is the home of all things that have ever been, and he has a reverent awe of the place. The house is a higher omnipotent being that he does not completely understand, nor can he. Why should he be expected to understand the will of a god?

Stairways adorned by magnificent architecture, Giovanni Battista Piranesi (1750)

In *The Poetics of Space*, Gaston Bachelard calls the house "our first universe, a real cosmos in every sense of the word. It is the human being's first world, before he is cast into the world." But what if it was the only world? What if there was no other world than the house you were born into? Would your perception of that space shift so that every square inch was a city block, every square foot a county? Would the kitchen and bathroom be separate principalities? Would there be windows or doors, and if so, what would be on the other side of them?

In *Room* (2015), Joy (Brie Larson) attempts to explain "outside" to her five-year-old son, Jack (Jacob Tremblay). She puts her hand up, indicating a "wall" and says, "Every wall has two sides, right?" He looks confused. In the magic "TV World" there are walls and forests and airplanes and cities, but that's just pretend stuff. But there in the real world, in Room, there is no wall. There is just here, and beyond that is "outer space." The mysterious "Old Nick" who visits his mother at night while he hides in Wardrobe is something magical and alien, partially here in the real world but able to travel out into the stratosphere where the TV people live.

Jack was born and raised inside a 12x12', soundproofed and vinyl-coated steel shed with a single skylight (through which he zoomed from outer space into his mother's belly). Until now, his fifth birthday, his mother hasn't had the heart to tell him the truth of his condition: that his mother was kidnapped when she was nineteen and "Old Nick" is not magical but an unemployed psychopath who has been raping her for the seven years she's been imprisoned. Jack doesn't know that Room is not the totality of the world but only a very, very, very small part of something much larger that he's never been allowed to see. He doesn't know there are more people in the world than just the two of them, but every morning Jack greets the objects in Room: "Good morning sink, good morning toilet, good morning rug…," with a seemingly innate need for community, for other people, and he treats them as such. Unlike the torture of solitary confinement, or the voluntary retreat of a hermit, Jack is blissfully unaware of what he's missing.

The film (like the book it's based on by Emma Donoghue) is narrated by Jack. He refers to Room as if it's the name of a place. I live in Brooklyn; he lives in Room. I was born in Cincinnati; he was born in Room. When Jack demands they get a dog, his mom trips up and says, "There's not enough room! I mean space. There's not enough space." It would be a bit like saying there's not enough Earth for a dog. After a harrowing escape devised by Joy, he attempts to explain to the police where he came from, that he wasn't *in* a house. "Room's not in a house," he says. Confused, the officer asks what Room *is* in. "Nothing. Room's inside."

For Jack, the world is divided into two states of place: inside and outside. The known world, reality, is *in*. Everything else, the unknown, the extraterrestrial, is *out*. After seeing cars and trees and other people, his world expands to include more than he could have imagined. Once Joy is home, he can now experience a house the way we understand it, and understands that there can be many rooms in one house, and that there are many houses in the world all with their own rooms. There are universes within universes.

But Jack wants to see his old home, Room, one last time. The threshold is blocked by crime scene tape, and all the objects that used to be his comrades — Rug, Table — are gone. It's much smaller to him now. But it's not just the scale that's changed, it's the very nature of the universe that's changed for him. "It's not Room now," he says. His mother sniffs the air. "You don't think so? It used to smell even staler. The door's open now, of course." Jack wonders if that's the difference. "Maybe it's not Room if Door's open."

Room and *Piranesi* both use private language as a metaphor for the condition of captivity of characters who have no idea they are captive at all. Piranesi's calendar system is unique to his experiences and where they occur ("The seventh day of the fifth month in the year the albatross came to the southwestern halls"). Our world is reflected in how and what we choose to define.

In *Room*, Jack's use of language developed organically based on his perception of the world as he knew it, and his mother protected him from the horror of his circumstances until he was old enough to know the truth. In Yorgos Lanthimos' *Dogtooth* (2009) the parents instill in their children a mortal fear of an imagined danger to keep them captive and weaponize language to maintain control. The film fittingly opens with a vocabulary lesson:

> *Motorway = a very strong wind*
> *Excursion = a very resistant material*
> *Sea = a leather armchair with wooden arms like we have*
> *in our living room*

The students, three teenage siblings, sit in the bathroom and listen obediently, if a bit bored. Later we learn "phone" is a saltshaker and "zombie" is a small yellow flower. "Pussy" is a big light; "vulva" is a keyboard. Theirs is a customized vocabulary devised by their parents, who are clearly making it up as they go along. The only objects or experiences they know are the things inside the perimeter of their house and what their parents have told them exist. They've never stepped beyond the backyard. Every new word they may inadvertently be exposed to from the outside world is assigned a new meaning by their parents. Any curiosity about the world beyond the high hedged fence surrounding their property is mitigated through language. There's no television, no radio, and the telephone is kept locked in their parents' bedroom. The only movies they've seen are home movies, replays of themselves turning their home into an echo chamber for the meticulously contrived existence created for them. Even product labels are removed from bottles.

In an effort to protect their children, the parents have

created a completely contained ecosystem which no outside influence can contaminate (apart from the woman the father pays to have sex with his teenage son, to stymie any incestuous experimentation). The kids know there is a world beyond the fence that encloses them, it is just a very, very dangerous one. Their father is the only one allowed to leave the property, and even then, only when inside the safety of his car. As Mark Fisher writes, "The outside must be totally pathologized: the children have to become literally xenophobic, terrified of everything that lies beyond the limits of their 'protected' enclave."[7]

There's a rampant narcissism in the father's over-protection, in his belief that everything outside of the world he created is dangerous or wicked. There are all sorts of ways parents try to stave off the big bad world for as long as they can before the chicks leap out of the nest, but the hope is that they will leave at some point. Home is supposed to be a place of shelter from harm, but "sheltered" is a pejorative. To be sheltered is to be naive, unknowing, and ill-equipped to survive in the world. It is to be forced into an infantilized state.

On 20 November, 1970, in the kitchen of 6722 Golden West Avenue in Arcadia, California, sixty-nine-year-old Clark Wiley left two suicide notes before shooting himself in the head. One was to his eighteen-year-old son, which read, "Be a good boy, I love you." The other was not *to* his daughter, but *about* her, and read, "The world will never understand." Clark Wiley also kept his daughter sheltered from the world under a perverse idea of protecting her from harm, but he killed himself before he was to appear in court and explain why he did what he did. And he's right: I don't understand.

The house on Golden West Avenue looks like a typical

ranch house from the outside. Almost. If one were to look closely, they would see all the windows had been covered or tightly shuttered. Photos of the exterior of the house show flat white where the glass would be, the garage door closed, even the car covered with a tarp. It is aggressively beige, trying too hard not to be noticed. It was a house never meant to be entered, and inside was a girl who was never meant to come out. But on 4 November, 1970, Irene Wiley defied her oppressively controlling husband, left her sealed up house, and brought her daughter with her. Irene was nearly blind and went to the welfare offices in Temple City to apply for disability benefits, but she walked into the social services office by mistake. She hadn't intended to rescue the girl, but that's what happened. Social workers saw a small, emaciated child, hunched over behind her mother, with her arms oddly bent. Something was very wrong. She was drooling and spitting as if unable to swallow. Unable to fully extend her limbs, she walked with a strange halting gait the doctors would call her "bunny hop." They thought she was about six or seven and possibly autistic because of her lack of speech. She could recognize a few words: she knew "red" and "yellow," but she could only speak two phrases blended into single words: "stopit" and "nomore."[8]

They called her Genie, and she was not six or seven, but almost thirteen. She had never learned to speak because no one ever spoke to her. If language is a reflection of one's environment, there was a void in Genie's language because her home was a void. She spent her life locked in an empty dark room with almost no human interaction. She was not yet two years old, her age still measured in months, when she was strapped into a homemade toddler-sized straight jacket and bound to a potty chair all day, every day. At night she was confined in another custom-made device, a sleeping bag, so she couldn't move the metal screen covering the crib.

The room had two almost entirely blacked-out windows. One was left slightly open; although the house was well away from the street and other houses, you could see the side of a neighboring house. She occasionally heard environmental sounds or a neighboring child practicing the piano, another cruel torture. Because she had no visual stimulation in that dark room, she couldn't focus her eyes beyond twelve feet.

She was sometimes allowed to "play" with a plastic raincoat, an old *TV Guide*, or a thread spool. She was fed mostly mushy food that her father forced her to eat so quickly she would choke. If she made any noise, she was beaten with a board. Clark was intolerant of noise. There was no television or radio in the house. His wife and son were forbidden to talk to Genie, and spoke in whispers outside of her door so she wouldn't overhear. A particularly disturbing outcome of this was that Genie seemed unable to cry.

"Child abuse" feels tame, too pedestrian a term for Clark's crime. Genie is often referred to as "feral," but that doesn't feel right either. Feral suggests something wild, a child out in the wilderness, raised by wolves, made to fend for themselves alone in the world. For Genie, there was no other world. She was not wild, she had been violently and sadistically suppressed, and she wasn't alone: she was egregiously ignored. When I first heard about Genie, it was incomprehensible to me. It's still incomprehensible to me, to grow up unmoving and alone in a small dark room, to live in darkness and silence, to be born only to return to a crueler, colder, and more painful womb.

The first twenty months of her life were relatively normal. She was healthy, if perhaps a bit small for her age. She had hip dysplasia, so she started walking late, and at fourteen months a pediatrician suggested Genie might have a learning disability, despite having no evidence to back up his claim. This careless diagnosis may have condemned her. When Clark's mother was killed in a hit-and-run accident outside of her home, he spiraled into a permanent state of despair and rage that he would take out on his whole family. He beat his nearly blind wife, Irene. He beat his then five-year-old son. He quit his job, moved his family into his mother's house, and retreated from the world. He believed Genie's imagined disability made her particularly vulnerable, and that by keeping her out of the world he was protecting her.

Clark Wiley seemed unsure what to do with a home, its purpose got lost somewhere down the line. Clark was obsessed with his mother, and like Ed Gein and Norman Bates, he saved her bedroom untouched and locked as a shrine. The room for Genie (it's hard to call it Genie's room, since that would imply some ownership, some autonomy in the space) was a prison cell meant only for her. The rest of the family lived in the living room. Clark slept in a recliner, the mother at the kitchen table, and the brother on the floor. The bedrooms were left for the dead and the nearly dead, with the rest of his family squatting in between the two. Since Clark never bothered to explain what the "world would never understand," we can only speculate (if he's worth the effort of speculation.) He believed that Genie would only live to be twelve. He even promised his wife that if she lived past that age, he would let her go (he would renege on that promise). He seemed to be waiting for, counting on, her death, willing to put in only the least amount of effort to keep her alive.

The story of Genie's rescue, the strange tiny girl hiding behind her mother in a social services office, is known. The battle for her guardianship and care as she was shuffled between scientists, teachers, parents, and foster parents is well documented. What's not known, what I wish I knew, was what it was like for her to leave that room. Before she even stepped outside, what would it have been like for her to see her space expand, out of the room, through the hall, past the kitchen and the living room, until finally past the threshold of her front door? Before she even got to the welfare office, Genie had been outside for the first time since she was twenty months old, almost thirteen years. I want to know what her first time inhaling fresh air felt like, her first time seeing sunlight, experiencing the various surfaces under her feet: wood, tile, concrete, grass. Her first time seeing, hearing anything, anyone else. Was it all a numbing blur? Was she terrified or delighted? Did she have any idea that all of this was out here?

Piranesi is not the character's real name. He doesn't remember what happened to his old one. Genie is not her real name either. It's the name given to her by those who found her to protect her anonymity. Piranesi's namesake, Giovanni Battista Piranesi, was an eighteenth-century Italian architect and artist famous for his fantastic etchings of imagined prisons, labyrinthian and immense. Genie, a magical being, lived in a bottle waiting for someone to set her free.

In *Dogtooth*, the siblings are aware of airplanes since one will occasionally fly over their house. The parents, with almost playful mischief, toss a toy plane in the grass announcing one has fallen from the sky. Their children have no frame of reference for a real plane, no concept of the distance or that there may be people inside those metal containers in the sky. For after-dinner entertainment, the father plays Frank

Sinatra's *Fly Me to the Moon*, but tells them it's a recording of their grandfather. He translates the lyrics as:

> *Dad loves us. Mom loves us. Do we love them? Yes, we do. My house, you are beautiful. I love you and will never leave you.*

The children smile warmly, basking in parental affection, safe in their confinement, listening to a song comparing love to flying away without even knowing.

Sheltering in place

"We're all indoor cats now."
— Karen Kilgariff, *My Favorite Murder*

One thing I've learned about myself is that I have no problem being under quarantine. In the early days of COVID-19, before N95 masks became a regular order on Amazon, before "social distancing" was a normal thing people said, like everyone else, I scoured websites on how to make your own mask without a sewing machine. I looked up how to make homemade hand sanitizer. When I did venture out for groceries, there was a whole decontamination process of wiping down boxes of cereal before they crossed the threshold into the pure space of my kitchen. Outside was the constant wailing of ambulances down my street, one after another. The turbulence of the final year of a Trump presidency, glass façades of the Apple Store elegantly covered in gleaming white plywood to protect it from George Floyd protesters, the unprecedented weirdness of the world were all *out there*, but inside was just fine. I got into plants, most of which are still thriving, thank you very much.

Joseph Masco, in *Life Underground: Building the Bunker Society*, writes: "The bunker is a transportation architecture, but rather than transport bodies and material through space, it transports them through time." Once someone goes into the bunker, they don't come out. Once the door closes, anyone outside stays outside and anyone inside stays inside. The bunker is a home frozen in time, and the world that you leave behind is expected to be very different from the one you eventually step back out into. COVID felt very much like that. When we left our offices, unsure when we would be back, we said, "See you on the other side," uncertain of when or what the other side would be.

As home, work, and play were flattened under one roof, we joked about time having no meaning anymore, of the days, weeks, years all blending into one brain-foggy haze. Time stood still inside or slowed down (Or maybe sped up?). My own marker for delineating between time spent at work and at home was slippers. I had "work" slippers, a little stiffer, with a harder sole, and after five o'clock I would change into my softer, cozier "home" slippers, moving from the computer at my desk to the laptop on my couch in front of the television. The first thing I reached for in the morning was my phone, and it was the last thing I put down at night, starting and ending my day with an endless scroll. The border between work and leisure was dictated by the size of the glowing screen I stared into, watching other people on Instagram doing the same thing I was. It was a rare time when everyone (almost) was doing the exact same thing, at the same time, using the same technology as we collectively adapted to life inside.

Host, directed by Rob Savage, came out in 2020, right at peak pandemic, and begins the way many of us spent our days and nights: on Zoom. We see the program's interface and hear the sound of soft mouse clicks on the orange "new meeting" button, then the blue "join with computer audio" button. We hear the sound of tape being removed from the camera, revealing the host, Haley (Haley Bishop), sitting at a desk, her face with the slack expression of someone who doesn't know yet that they're being watched. Jemma (Jemma Moore) joins and her head pops up next to the other woman's, and after some technical difficulty, they exchange niceties and go back to their phones to wait until someone they like better joins. One by one, the screen fills with a grid of faces: Emma (Emma Louise Webb), Caroline (Caroline Ward), Radina (Radina Drandova), and Teddy (Edward Linard) in their respective bedrooms, kitchens, and living rooms. We see the racks of hanging laundry, the unmade beds and cluttered kitchen counters of ordinary personal spaces. They've been doing this a while, they have quarantine down pat, it's not even much of a conversation anymore. There's a bit of gossip about Radina moving in with her boyfriend for lockdown. Caroline shows off her clever background video of herself meandering around her room, they each have a drink of choice, but the virtual bonding activity this time is a séance, which works a bit too well.

Unlike the typical found-footage horror (*Blair Witch Project*, *Paranormal Activity*, *V/H/S*), in which previously recorded material is discovered, *Host* is found footage created in real time. The tool bar of the app remains on the bottom of the screen for the duration, and our view is fixed until a character moves and takes their laptop with them. We see the space of the apartments and houses behind them, we see the void of an open door down the hall, a point on the screen from which we've been trained to expect a jump scare. Every now and then I would glance at the "participants" icon at the bottom of the frame, waiting for it to bump up a number, a little indication that something else has entered the meeting. While we may all have had innocuous experiences like those that usually begin horror movies (a weekend vacation…) it feels different watching a horror movie in which the characters are doing very much what *we're* doing, watching a screen, in the same way and at the same time we're doing in, using the same technology.

As they look into their screens, each face illuminated by a candle, taking a drink whenever the medium says, "Astral plane," they visualize themselves being in the same place, sitting together in a circle, and call out to a spirit. The activities are temporarily paused when Seylan, the medium, excuses herself to open the door for her take-out delivery. Jemma is getting a bit bored and pretends to have a supernatural experience with the ghost of a dead boy she invented on the spot, unwittingly inviting an evil spirit into the chat, creating a ghost where there wasn't one before. While Jemma might have created this entity, it spread across the Wi-Fi, entering every home on the screen, a virtual demon unbound by a single place or person.

Since each character is experiencing their own terrors in their own home, we are watching five separate haunted house movies in one. Caroline's head is smashed repeatedly on her laptop, resulting in a garbled message in the chat. Haley is thrown and dragged about her apartment. The dead body of Radina's boyfriend drops from the floor above. Teddy, who dipped out for a bit with his girlfriend and missed most of the action, ends up on fire. Each character is watching the others' nightmares while experiencing their own. They cover their eyes, pull their hoodies down while staring into the screen, as if they're watching a scary movie (or rather five scary movies at the same time). After thirty minutes the pop-up ten-minute warning appears on the screen asking, "Running out of time?" Someone (or something) thankfully hits the "Upgrade Now" button, removing the pesky forty-minute time limit, both releasing and heightening the tension. The view shifts from full-screen "speaker" view to gallery mode as the grid dwindles screen by screen until someone (or something) finally ends the meeting. The end credits are a scroll through the list of participants window. In a nice touch, the sound designer is the only one with their camera off. The movie is fifty-six minutes, just about the length of time I can deal with a Zoom meeting. *Host* is best watched on a laptop. I also recommend noise canceling headphones.

The movie was shot during lockdown in the actors' real homes with their phones Velcro-ed to their laptops. The wardrobe is their wardrobe, the lighting limited to the lighting in their apartments. Savage sent all the actors thin fishing wire and gave them tutorials on old-school special effects. "We beat the shit out of all their houses."[9]

My world, like a lot of people's during quarantine, was condensed down to my apartment, and my life coalesced on the screen. Work and play all happened in the same place, on the same device. Work was on Zoom, weddings were on Zoom, final goodbyes were on Zoom. (I've formulated a conspiracy theory that COVID-19 was developed and released by Zoom Video Communications, Inc., but you didn't hear it from me.) So why not a haunting on Zoom? It makes sense that the monster of our times would manifest through the communal experience of a video call in the comfort of our own homes, that the harbinger of doom would be the very tool we use to connect to other people, to simulate human interaction when we're keeping six feet apart.

A while ago, I downloaded a horror virtual reality app. I panned my phone across my dark room, waiting for something to appear. I will admit, I had to turn it off. I knew there wasn't a demon crawling on my ceiling, but it creeped me out too much to see it visualized so clearly. Savage says, "As a horror filmmaker all you want to do is to make people scared of their own home."[10] During the pandemic, before we got accustomed to sticking medical swabs up our noses, before the vaccine, when the hospitals were overrun, when the number of deaths a day kept ticking up and up, you couldn't ask for a better venue for a horror movie than your own home, your guaranteed safe space.

My House

"Almost any house caught unexpectedly or at an odd angle can turn a deeply humorous look on a watching person; even a mischievous little chimney or a dormer like a dimple, can catch up a beholder with a sense of fellowship; but a house arrogant and hating, never off guard, can only be evil."

— *The Haunting of Hill House,* Shirley Jackson

Not all of the houses in my collection are haunted. Some are arrogant: the Tanz Academy, the Sowden House. Some are hateful: the Unabomber Cabin, Ed Gein's house. Not all of them are evil, some are merely mischievous: Sarah Winchester's house, Boro's house. But the haunted ones are my favorite. Regardless of their architectural make and model, no matter when, where, or why they were constructed, from the most opulent to the most humble, every home has the potential for haunting. The haunted house is the most intimate kind of horror because our homes are our second bodies, the epidermis of our externalized selves, our protective shell. Monsters, demons, and mad serial killers may come after us, but where do we run to for safety? Home.

I have had fourteen homes in my life, and I use that term loosely. I would consider any place where I stayed long enough to put something on the wall as home. Anywhere I took the time to mark the space as mine, however temporarily. Only one I can say may have been haunted.

The Webster Apartments, a *Bosom Buddy*-style hotel for women, was my first home in New York City after leaving Ohio. Founded in 1932 as a place for single working women in the city, it's a throwback to another time, when a job was merely a stepping-stone before marriage and a house in Westchester. There was a curfew, men were restricted to the ground floor, and there were multiple sewing rooms. The walls of my room were painted with decades of layers of white paint, no doubt reducing the original square footage a centimeter or so. There was a twin-sized, metal-framed bed with a small table and a hardbacked chair, a black-and-white television I don't remember working, and a fan mounted to the wall. There was a sink, but the bathroom was shared. My first night, I bought a cheap bottle of red and sat on the sill of my open window smoking a cigarette and admiring the view of a brick wall. It was fantastic. I wasn't home yet, but I was on my way. My second home, in the East Village on Third Street, across from the old Hell's Angels bar (the safest street in NYC), was the first home that felt, for lack of a better word, wrong. Maybe it was the fact that there was no sink in the bathroom, so we had to brush our teeth in the kitchen. My room, behind French doors I slid open and closed, was probably a parlor of some kind back in the day when it was a single-family home, before it was chopped up and stitched back together as something else.

For some houses, their history lingers longer than it should, their pasts stubborn, like the decades of dust compounded in the corners of the molding. But new homes aren't immune. Modernism isn't exempt from what Anthony Vider calls the "architectural uncanny." A new house may not be "haunted by the weight of tradition and the imbrications of generations of family drama," but the glass-walled lair and the skyscraping condo provide a clean slate, a blank canvas, to inspire state-of-the-art maleficence from their tenants. Sometimes houses are completely innocent bystanders, inanimate structures as they were meant to be, their reputations tarnished by human monstrosity.

So we never bring an old broom to a new house. We have houses blessed, burn sage to clean out the old energy, dislodge the old bad vibes, and do what we can to erase any residual traces left behind. Then we paint the front door haint blue to make sure the evil doesn't come back. But some houses refuse to settle.

British polymath Charles Babbage published *The Ninth Bridgewater Treatise* in 1837, in which he speculated that spoken words could leave permanent impressions in the atmosphere. He said, "The air itself is one vast library." In the 1930s, then president of the Society for Psychical Research H. H. Price believed that emotional traces from the past were carried in the "psychic ether" and implanted into trees, water, rocks, and whatever other solid object happened to be in their way. In his book *Ghost and Ghoul*, written in 1962, archeologist turned paranormal researcher T. C. Lethbridge argued that certain substances can absorb the energy of traumatic events and imprint an image of those events on the material itself, an accidental recording, like a shadow burned into concrete. But it was a 1972, BBC made-for-tv movie that would give these theories a name.

In *The Stone Tape*, the Ryan Electric Products company is in search of an innovative new recording medium, and have set up their research team in a Victorian mansion. However, their would-be server room has been hijacked by the ghost of a maid who fell to her death from a flight of steps in 1892. Her screams repeat over and over, the same length, the same pitch, a terrified screech rewound and played back. Jill Greeley, the hyper-sensitive, swoon-prone computer programmer, finds the idea of this spirit lingering, "of there being nothing left of you, but just enough to repeat the worst moment of your life over and over again," rather horrifying. Peter Brock, the arrogant and abrasive team leader, insists that there is no consciousness in the phenomenon, no awareness of its condition, that there is no ghost at all, just the room itself projecting the image of a traumatic death. Just a "dead mechanism."

The so-called Stone Tape theory (or the theory of residual haunting) provides a simple and elegant explanation for why ghosts walk through walls. While alive, we take the same paths over and over in our homes: bedroom to bathroom, living room to kitchen, upstairs to the attic, downstairs to the basement. We repeat the pattern of our daily lives, and the longer we inhabit a space, the more entrenched those paths become. But then we die, and if we have the misfortune of a tragic death, perhaps the tread of our troubled ghostly boots leave prints behind, a phantom desire path over carpet, hardwood, and tile. Perhaps the scent of trauma lingers in the air and settles into the brick, or electromagnetic energy etches itself into the limestone like a Uri Geller thoughtography print or Samara psychically imprinting her misery on to a VHS tape to be copied over and over.

But time passes, houses change hands, and new people move in, crossing predetermined pathways. Chairs and sofas are put in new places, rooms are added, taken away, or given new purposes; walls come down, and new ones go up. The floorplan changes, but the recording stays the same. The ghost walks the path they know, regardless of what new obstruction might be in their way. This theory feels logical, even plausible, because it suggests a formerly human life engaging in human behavior regardless of incorporeality. It's what we expect in a haunting. This was not my ghost.

I hesitate to say I had a ghost, because it seems ridiculous to call it that. A ghost is supposed to be a wispy, translucent suggestion of a human figure; a shadow cast from thin air; a hint of movement in the corner of the eye; a glowing orb caught in the flash of a camera; a blurry, smoky gossamer mark across the screen. We know what ghosts do: They pace the floor above us with disembodied stomps or ominous squeaks on the stairs. They open and close doors and kitchen cabinets. They mess with the electrical system, drawing energy from light fixtures and batteries, causing floor lamps to flicker and video cameras to die. Ghosts push planchettes across Ouija boards, whisper their names in EVP devices and spirit boxes. They suck the warmth out of the air where they float, dropping the temperature in small, localized spots. There is a playbook ghosts follow in horror movies, and we have expectations of how they should behave. This was not my ghost.

I was living in a studio apartment on the second floor of a nondescript, redbrick, six-floor walk-up in Prospect Heights, Brooklyn. Built around 1910, it was old enough to have some history, but there was nothing particularly unique about it, nothing interesting, and you'd expect a haunted house to have some character or a least a back story.

This occurred around Halloween (I know, I know, I'm just saying), when I decided to scan and digitize the collection of snapshots I've accumulated from thrift shops and flea markets. Like houses, for a while I collected little bits of other people's memories, images of people probably long dead, often posing proudly in front of houses. I came home from work one night, checked my mailbox, and found that a screw holding the hinges had come undone and was sitting in the box. I screwed it back in and made a mental note to tighten it properly with a real screwdriver tomorrow. When I opened the door to my apartment and turned on the lights, I saw there was a mound of… stuff in the middle of the kitchen floor. A mound of debris, I suppose. It looked like the accumulation of months of sweepings in a neat mound about five inches in diameter and maybe one to one-and-a-half inches high. The ceiling was bare, and there was nothing spilling out from under the floorboards. Mixed in the pile of grey material was what looked like dry dog food (I don't have a dog) and a screw. I stared at it, trying to figure out how this pile of stuff could have made its way to the middle of my brightly lit and very clean (if I do say so myself) kitchen. I decided maybe it was a mouse trying to build a nest, grabbing materials from inside the walls and other people's apartments. But I'd seen rodent nests, and they're usually made of substantive things: bits of fabric, paper, string, and pillow stuffing. This was just dust and dust-like stuff. Plus, mice don't build nests in brightly lit, open spaces. I swept up the pile into the dustpan and tossed it in the garbage, remembering that no one has keys to my apartment, not even the superintendent. My brain had no place to go with this, nothing to cling to that would spark fear, just confusion. I might have scanned a few more photos before going to bed that night.

The next day, I came home from work and the pile was back. Including the screw. I stood looking back and forth from the pile to the trash, from the ceiling to the pile, for at least five minutes. I looked up and around the walls and surveyed my kitchen in a state of what I can only describe as annoyed befuddlement. I looked in the garbage from the day before, but of course there was nothing really there to see. I swept this pile up slower this time, and speaking out loud, not really knowing who or what I was addressing, said, "I'm just going to clean this up. No offense!" I called a friend who lived nearby, who insisted I stay with her. No, I said. I was fine. I don't think I was fine, but I didn't understand what I was feeling. I do remember a kind of numbing confusion, fear just below the surface. But I did put the old photos away and might have apologized, just in case.

The next day, I came home from work, turned on the light, and the mound was back. It wasn't exactly the same as before, it was a bit smaller this time and there was no screw. I wasn't so much afraid as awed by all this. I even felt a little thrill that something genuinely bizarre was happening to me. The fourth day the mound was much, much smaller, then that was it. After that, no more dust mounds. I told myself that it must have been some very insistent and very confused rodent, but I didn't really believe it. I wish it was something more obvious: a book flying across the room, cabinet doors opening and closing, the lights flashing on and off. But this is what I got. It didn't feel malevolent. I didn't feel threatened. It was just really, really, really weird. I didn't abandon my apartment like the Lutz family. This didn't seem Ed and Lorraine Warren worthy. In bed, I would lie in the dark staring into the empty void of my kitchen, that thin fear rising to the surface, waiting to catch a glimpse of something, a faint spectral mist of a figure with a broom or at least an orb. I listened for the sounds of tiny rustling claws across the tile floor. I heard nothing but my next-door neighbors having sex and the occasional thump of a dropped shoe above me. I workshopped theories with friends and co-workers, but the only thing we came up with was a very persistent mouse with poor survival skills.

There is one other thing (and I'm reluctant to mention it because it ventures into lingering spirit territory, and I find the thought of my consciousness sticking around for decades after my death depressing; I can't image having any "unfinished business" after death that would require me to stay in a studio apartment in Brooklyn for all eternity). Below me, on the first floor, an old woman died in her apartment. I never met her, I never saw her, I never knew she existed until I saw various uniformed people coming out of her apartment one day and was hit with the smell. It was horrible and unmistakable. I hesitate to mention it, because I cannot remember when this happened, whether it was before or after the Pile. Was her apartment *directly* below mine? I don't remember. I never put the two incidents together at the time, because the thought of a ghost of a dead woman materializing little piles of debris in my kitchen is absurd. Just as thinking the spirits of the people in the snapshots were somehow offended by my digitizing is absurd. But my instinct is to do just that, to create motive and intent for the dead, to give them a narrative. We expect haunted houses to have stories, to say something about the lives of people that we never knew; we expect a haunted house to have a life like ours, or at least one that we can recognize. We need a reason for a haunting, to give the paranormal some normalcy, to center the living in a story that isn't about them.

If you were to ask me if I think ghosts are real, I'd say, "Probably." We call them ghosts because we don't know what they are yet, but we probably will someday. There will be someone in the future who will know why we hear footsteps above us when there is no one there, why books get tossed off shelves, or glasses break on their own, why mounds of dust materialize on kitchen floors. Someday someone will figure out the science of the haunted house and we will have reasonable explanations for those things that go bump in the night. There will be real-life ghostbusters, spectral exterminators hired to clean our houses. There will be spirit Roombas and inconspicuously designed ghost traps to stick on the floorboards. Instagram and TikTok will be filled with life hacks for dealing with the dead. Property values will rise or fall depending on whether the ghost is considered an asset or a liability. Someday, there will be treatments for sick houses, but hopefully not soon, because haunted-house stories still make the best movies.

Unabomber Gingerbread Cabin,
author (2019)

Image Credits

The Unhappy House

Page X : Grant Groberg, 2006.

American Houses

Page 5: magazineart.org.

Page 6: Gottscho-Schleisner, Inc, photographer. Levittown houses. Peg Brennan, residence at 25 Winding Lane. New York, New York State Levittown, United States, 1958. www.loc.gov/item/2018729983/.

Page 23: *His House* (2020), directed by Remi Weekes. Credit: Regency Enterprises / Album, Alamy Stock Photo.

Brutal Houses

Page 30: *The Black Cat* (1934), directed by Edgar G. Ulmer / TCD/Prod.DB / Alamy Stock Photo.

Page 33: *House on Haunted Hill* (1959), directed by William Castle, Allied Artists.

Page 35: Sowden House, Franklin Avenue, Los Angeles, California, 1933. Historic American Buildings Survey, Creator, Lloyd Wright, W W Moore, Sponsor Southern California Coordinating Committee for Historic Preservation, Sponsor University of Southern California,

Robert C Giebner, Esther McCoy, et al., Rand, Marvin, photographer. www.loc.gov/item/ca0267/.

Page 41: Cité Radieuse, Le Corbusier, Dino Fracchia / Alamy Stock Photo.

Page 48: Pruitt-Igoe resident Etta McCowan, April 1967, © Floyd Bowser/St Louis Post-Dispatch / ZUMAPRESS. com

Page 49: The second, widely televised demolition of a Pruitt-Igoe building that followed the March 16 demolition, U.S. Department of Housing and Urban Development, April 1972. Wikimedia.

Page 55: *A Clockwork Orange* (1971), directed by Stanley Kubrick. Collection Christophel © Warner Bros / Hawk films.

Page 55: Southmere estate, Thamesmead, London, UK, 2015, Cecilia Colussi Stock / Alamy Stock Photo.

Page 59: *The Island Nobody Knows*, Philip Johnson and John Burgee, 1969, The Metropolitan Museum of Art.

Page 59: The Landing (Eastman Apartments), author photo, 2024.

Witch Houses

Page 71: *Häxan* (1922), directed by Benjamin Christensen.

Page 73: Spadena House, Kafziel, 2011.

Page 73: *Baba Yaga's Hut*, Ivan Bilibin, 1899.

Page 75: *Suspiria* (1977) directed by Dario Argento / Prod DB Â© Seda Spettacoli /DR / Alamy Stock Photo.

Page 80: *Hansel and Gretel in front of the witch's house*, Otto Kubel, 1930.

Page 82: *Gretel and Hansel* (2020) directed by Oz Perkins /

Automatik Entertainment / Orion Pictures / Bron Studios / Alamy Stock Photo.

Mad Houses

Page 102: Unabomber Cabin, Newseum, Washington D.C., author photo, 2019.

Page 107: *House by the Railroad*, Edward Hopper, 1925, The Metropolitan Museum of Art.

Page 108: *Psycho* (1960), directed by Alfred Hitchcock, Paramount / Alamy Stock Photo.

Page 111: *The Addams Family* (1964), Allstar Picture Library Limited. / Alamy Stock Photo

Page 115: *The Home of the Benders: The Machinery of Murder, History, Romance, and Philosophy of Great American Crimes*, by Frank Triplett, 1884

Page 121: Aladdin Houses kit catalog, North American Construction Company, 1915. Internet Archive.

Page 123: Home of serial killer Ed Gein in Plainfield in Wisconsin, 1957, Getty Images, Bettmann.

Little Houses

Page 134: Dining room of an antique doll's house, Custom Life Science Images, Alamy Stock Photo.

Page 135: Barbie's Dreamhouse, Stephen Chung, 1962, Alamy Stock Photo.

Page 143: *Hereditary* (2018), directed by Ari Aster, Reid Chavis - PalmStar Media - Windy Hill Pictures, Alamy Stock Photo.

Page 148: Case in the *Nutshell Studies*, model of "An Unexplained Double Murder," Edwin Remsberg / Alamy Stock Photo.

Forever Houses

Page 161: *Popular Science Monthly,* March 1951, Collection Philippe Clement / Alamy Stock Photo.

Page 163: *Cloverfield Lane* (2016), directed by Dan Trachtenberg, Moviestore Collection / Alamy Stock Photo.

Page 170: *Stairways adorned by magnificent architecture*, Giovanni Battista Piranesi, 1750, Heritage Image Partnership Ltd / Alamy Stock Photo.

My House

Page 195: Unabomber Gingerbread Cabin, author (2019)

Bibliography

American Houses

Allen, Lewis, director. *The Uninvited*. Paramount Pictures, Inc., 1944.

Amenábar, Alejandro, director. *The Others*. Dimension Films, 2001.

Angelini, Giorgio, director. *Owned: A Tale of Two Americas*, 2018.

Bachelard, Gaston. *The Poetics of Space*. Beacon Press, 1994.

Churchwell, Sarah Bartlett. *Behold, America: The Entangled History of "America First" and "The American Dream"*. Basic Books, 2018.

Clark, Clifford Edward. *The American Family Home: 1800–1960*. University of North Carolina Press, 1987.

Comaroff, Joshua, and Ong Ker-Shing. *Horror in Architecture*. ORO editions, 2018.

Cornwell, Peter, director. *The Haunting in Connecticut*. Lionsgate Films, 2009.

Cullen, Jim. *The American Dream: A Short History of an Idea That Shaped a Nation*. Oxford University Press, 2006.

Derrickson, Scott, director. *Sinister*. Lionsgate, 2012.

Després, Carole. "The Meaning of Home: literature review and directions for future research and theoretical development." *Journal of Architectural and Planning Research*. 8, no. 2 (1991): 96–115.

Dezember, Ryan. *Underwater: How Our American Dream of Homeownership Became a Nightmare*. Thomas Dunne Books, 2020.

Dickey, Colin. *Ghostland: An American History in Haunted Places*. Penguin Books, 2017.

Forrest, Ray and Yosuke Hirayama. "The Financialisation of the Social Project: Embedded Liberalism, Neoliberalism and Home Ownership." *Urban Studies*. 52 (2014): 233–44

Freud, Sigmund. *The Uncanny*. Penguin Books, 2003.

Goodman, Laurie S., and Christopher Mayer. "Homeownership and the American Dream." *Journal of Economic Perspectives*. 32, no.1 (Winter 2018): 31–58.

Letho, Steve. *American Murder Houses*. Berkley, 2015.

Maggio, John, director. *Panic: The Untold Story of the 2008 Financial Crisis*. Vice News, 2018.

Obama, Barack. "Remarks by the President on Responsible Homeownership." National Archives and Records Administration. August 6, 2013.

Peele, Jordan, director. *Us*. Universal Pictures, 2019.

Pliny the Younger. *Letters of Pliny the Younger*. Hinds, Noble & Eldredge, 1900.

Rosenberg, Stuart, director. *The Amityville Horror*. American International Pictures, 1979.

Riccobono, Jack, director. *Amityville: An Origin Story*. MGM+, 2023.

Schudson, Michael. "American Dreams." *American Literary History* 16, no. 3 (2004): 566–73.

Sixsmith, Judith. "The Meaning of Home: An Exploratory Study of Environmental Experience." *Journal of Environmental Psychology*. 6 (1986): 281–98.

Stambovsky v. Ackley, 169 A.D.2d 254, 572 N.Y.S.2d 672 (N.Y. App. Div. 1991).

Tobey, Ronald, Charles Wetherell, and Jay Brigham. "Moving Out and Settling In: Residential Mobility, Home Owning, and the Public Enframing of Citizenship, 1921–1950." *The American Historical Review*. 95, no. 5 (1990): 1395–422.

Walpole, Horace. *The Castle of Otranto: A Gothic Story*. Oxford World's Classics, 2014.

Wan, James, director. *The Conjuring*. Warner Bros. Pictures, 2015.

Weekes, Remi, director. *His House*. Netflix, 2020.

Brutal Houses

Ballard, J. G. *High-Rise: A Novel*. W. W. Norton & Company, 2012.

Banham, Reyner. *The New Brutalism*, Architectural Press, 1966.

Burgee, John, and Philip Johnson. *The Island Nobody Knows*. New York State Urban Development Corporation, New York, 1969.

Castle, William, director. *House on Haunted Hill*. Allied Artists, 1959.

Cilento, Karen. "Frank Lloyd Wright's Textile Houses." *ArchDaily*, 14 September, 2010.

Cinema Tyler, "The Real Futuristic Art and Locations Kubrick Found for a Clockwork Orange." YouTube, 26 May, 2020.

Coleman, Nathaniel. "The Problematic of Architecture and Utopia." *Utopian Studies*. 25, no. 1 (2014): 1–22.

Comerio, Mary C. "Pruitt Igoe and Other Stories." *JAE*. 34, no. 4 (1981): 26–31.

Cronenberg, David, director. *Shivers*. Cinépix Film Properties, 1975.

Cunningham, Chris, director. *Come to Daddy: Aphex Twin*. Warp Records, 1997.

Drennan, William R. *Death in a Prairie House: Frank Lloyd Wright and the Taliesin Murders*. Terrace Books, 2007.

Easton, Kenneth. "Views on Le Corbusier's Unite d'Habitation." *Architectural Review*, 8 May, 1951.

Frampton, Kenneth. *Modern Architecture: A Critical History*. Thames & Hudson, 1985.

Freidrichs, Chad, director. *The Pruitt-Igoe Myth*. First Run Features, 2011.

Gans, Herbert J. "The High-Rise Fallacy." *Design Quarterly*, 157 (Autumn 1992): 24–8.

Gill, John Freeman. "…And on Roosevelt Island, Being Afraid, Really Afraid." *The New York Times*, 17 July, 2005.

Hanson, Kitty. "Welfare Island: Stepchild with Sordid Past." *Daily News*, 23 October, 1967.

Hatherley, Owen. *Militant Modernism*. Zero Books, 2009.

Hawthorne, Chris, director. "That Far Corner: Frank Lloyd Wright in Los Angeles." *Artbound*, pbs.org, 6 March, 2018.

Hazzard, Jago. "Thamesmead: A Town for the Twenty-First Century." YouTube, 16 April, 2021.

Heathcote, Edwin. "The Architecture of Horror Shifts from Gothic to Modernist." *Financial Times*, 1 April, 2022.

Hodel, Steve. *Black Dahlia Avenger: A genius for murder*. Harper, 2006.

Kroll, Andrew. "Architecture Classics: Unite d' Habitation / Le Corbusier." *ArchDaily*, 10 February, 2023.

Kubrick, Stanley, director. *A Clockwork Orange*. Warner Bros., 1971.

Lerner, Jesse. "The Complexities of Cross-Cultural Appropriation in Frank Lloyd Wright's Textile Block Houses." *Artbound*, PBS SoCal, 29 August, 2023.

O'Connor, Joanne. "From Kubrick's Dystopia to Creative Hub — London's New Town Is Reborn." *The Guardian*, 13 May, 2017.

Oppenheim, Chad, and Lair Gollin. *Radical Homes and Hideouts of Movie Villains*. Tra Publishing, 2019.

Meades, Jonathan. *Bunkers, Brutalism and Bloodymindedness: Concrete Poetry with Jonathan Meades*. BBC Four, February 16, 2014.

Miller, Joan. "Pruitt-Igoe: Survival in a Concrete Ghetto." *Social Work*. 12, no. 4 (1967): 3–13.

Parker, Ian. "Kanye West Bought an Architectural Treasure—Then Gave It a Violent Remix." *The New Yorker*, 10 June, 2024.

Rus, Mayer, and Jackie Nickerson. "Step inside Kim Kardashian West and Kanye West's Boundary-Defying Home." *Architectural Digest*, 3 February, 2020.

Salles, Walter, director. *Dark Water*. Buena Vista Pictures, 2005.

Sheridan, Sam, producer. *I Am the Night*. TNT, 2019.

Sippell, Margaux. "'I Am the Night' Team on Filming in the John Sowden House." *Variety*, 26 January, 2019.

Trufelman, Avery. "Hard to Love a Brute". *99% Invisible*, 12 August, 2015.

Ulmer, Edgar, director. *The Black Cat*. Universal Pictures, 1934.

Wheatley, Ben, director. *High-Rise*. StudioCanal, 2015.

Winston, Anne. "High Rise is 'not a criticism of post-war architecture'", *dezeen.com*, 25 March 2016. www.dezeen.com/2016/03/25/high-rise-movie-not-a-criticism-of-post-war-architecture-interview-director-ben-wheatley/

Zraick, Karen, and Ashley Wong. "'High-Rise Hell': N.Y.C. Skyscraper's Elevator Breakdowns Strand Tenants." *The New York Times*, 28 March, 2022.

Witch Houses

Antosca, Nick, creator. *Brand New Cherry Flavor*. Netflix, 2021.

Chollet, Mona. *In Defense of Witches: The Legacy of the Witch*

Hunts and Why Women Are Still on Trial. St. Martin's Press. 2022.

Denny, Frances F., and Pam Grossman. *Major Arcana: Portraits of Witches in America.* Andrews McMeel Publishing, 2020.

Eggener, Keith. "When Buildings Kill." *Places Journal,* 29 October, 2013.

Grossman, Pam. *Waking the Witch: Reflections on Women, Magic, and Power.* Gallery Books, 2019

Herring, Scott. *The Hoarders: Material Deviance in Modern American Culture.* University of Chicago Press, 2014.

Maysles, Albert and David Maysles, directors,. *Grey Gardens,* Portrait Films, 1975.

Mendelsohn, Hadley. "How a Famous Author Revived a Ruined Mansion Using Vintage Design Magazines", HouseBeautiful.com, 31 August, 2022.

Mendelsohn, Hadley. "How This Oceanfront Oasis Became the Most Infamous Mansion in the Hamptons". HouseBeautiful.com, 24 February, 2024.

McDonagh, Maitland. *Broken Mirrors/Broken Minds: The Dark Dreams of Dario Argento,* University of Minnesota Press, 2010.

Perkins, Osgood, director. *Gretel & Hansel.* United Artists Releasing, 2020

Sheehy, Gail. "The Secrets of Grey Gardens", *New York Magazine,* 10 January, 1972.

Sollée, Kristen J. *Witches, Sluts, Feminists: Conjuring the Sex Positive.* ThreeL Media, 2017.

Mad Houses

Blanco, Juan Ignacio. "The Bender Family". *Murderpedia.*

Burgmaier, Laurel Bower. *The Farm Crisis*. Iowa PBS, July 1, 2013.

Burns, Sarah. "Better for Haunts: Victorian Houses and the Modern Imagination". *American Art*. 26, No. 3 (Fall 2012): 2-25

Comaroff, Joshua, and Ong Ker-Shing. *Horror in Architecture: The Reanimated Edition*. University of Minnesota Press, 2024.

Drake, Phil. "Unabomber Ted Kaczynski Now Held in 'Alcatraz of the Rockies'". Helenair.com, 2 April, 2021.

Dressler, Jacob. "The History of The 'Texas Chainsaw Massacre' Farmhouse". *ScreenGeek*, 19 March, 2020.

Judge, Phoebe and Lauren Spohrer. "The Widow and the Winchester". *Criminal*, episode 107, February 1, 2019. Thisiscriminal.com/episode-107-the-widow-and-the-winchester-2-1-2019/

Ford, Richard. "Evil's Humble Home". *New York Times Magazine*, 1998.

French, Christine Madrid. *The Architecture of Suspense: The built world in the films of Alfred Hitchcock*. University of Virginia Press, 2022.

Harden, Tim. "Interview with Former Leatherface House Occupant". TexasChainsawMassacre.net, 2004.

Hitchcock, Alfred, director. *Psycho*, Paramount Pictures, 1960.

Ignoffo, Mary Jo. *Captive of the Labyrinth: Sarah L. Winchester, Heiress to the Rifle Fortune*. University of Missouri Press, 2010.

Jonusas, Susan. *Hell's Half-Acre: The Untold Story of the Benders, a Serial Killer Family on the American Frontier*. Penguin, 2023.

Library of America. "Hell Benders, or The Story of a Wayside Tavern". *Story of the Week*, 6 February 2022.

Lukić, Marko. *Geography of Horror: Spaces, Hauntings and the American Imagination*. Palgrave Macmillan, 2023.

Mikulee, Sven. "'Psycho': The Proto-Slasher That Brought

on a Revolution in Cinema". *Cinephilia & Beyond*, 14 June, 2020.

Mirabal, Marisa. "'Texas Chain Saw Massacre' Restaurant Grand Central Cafe Gets New Name Hooper's". *Eater Austin*, 14 March, 2023.

Rose, James. *The Texas Chain Saw Massacre*. Liverpool University Press, 2013.

Santa Clara University Digital Exhibits. "Winchester Mystery House as a Labyrinth." *Santa Clara University Digital Exhibits*. dh.scu.edu/exhibits/exhibits/show/winchester-mystery-house-as-a-/conclusion

Schechter, Harold. *Deviant*. Simon and Schuster, 2010.

Sodroski, Andrew, Jim Clemente, and Tony Gittelson, creators. *Manhunt: The Unabomber*. Discovery Channel, 2017.

Triplett, Frank. *History, Romance and Philosophy of Great American Crimes and Criminals*. Arkose Press, 2015.

Whitehead, John. director. *Death of the Dream: Farmhouses in the Heartland*. PBS, 2000.

Wigley, Mark. "Cabin Fever". *Perspecta 30, The Yale Architectural Journal*, 1999.

Wood, Anthony. "The Rise and Fall of the Great American Motel". *Smithsonian Magazine*, 30 June, 2017.

Worthington, Leah. *The Man Who Shot the Unabomber Cabin*. alumni.berkeley.edu, 30 November, 2023.

Little Houses

Beaumont, Charles. "The Miniature". *Twilight Zone*. 1963.

Botz, Corinne May, and Frances Glessner Lee. *The Nutshell Studies of Unexplained Death*. Monacelli Press, 2004.

Flynn, Gillian. *Sharp objects: A novel*. Broadway Books, 2018.

Garfield, Simon. *In Miniature: How small things illuminate the world*. Atria Books, 2019.

Glessner House. "Welcome to Glessner House". Glessnerhouse.org.

Glessner House Museum. "The Story of a House". Glessnerhouse.blogspot.com/

Lagacé, Rose. "Production Designer John Paino Gives Us an Insightful New Look at Sharp Objects". *Art Departmental*, 17 April, 2020.

Malerman, Josh. "The House of the Head". *Creepshow*. 2019.

Miller, Daniel, editor. *Home Possessions: Material Culture Behind Closed Doors*. Berg, 2001.

Mortimer, Adam Egypt, director. *Daniel Isn't Real*. Samuel Goldwyn Films, 2019.

Murphy, Nick, director. *The Awakening*. Studio Canal, 2011.

Stewart, Susan. *On Longing: Narratives of the miniature, the gigantic, the souvenir and the collection*. Duke University Press, 1993.

Tristram, Philippa. *Living Space: In Fact and Fiction*. Routledge, 1989.

Forever Houses

Belmont, Cynthia, and Angela Stroud. "Bugging Out: Apocalyptic Masculinity and Disaster Consumerism in Offgrid Magazine." *Feminist Studies*. 46, no. 2 (2020): 431–58.

Bishop, Thomas. *Every Home a Fortress: Cold War Fatherhood and the Family Fallout Shelter*. University of Massachusetts Press, 2020.

Donoghue, Emma. *Room*. Back Bay Books, 2010.

Fisher, Mark. "Dogtooth: The Family Syndrome". *Film Quarterly*. 64, No. 4 (Summer 2011:) 22–7.

Garrett, Bradley. *Bunker: Building for the End Times.* Scribner, 2020.

Garrett, Bradley. "Doomsday preppers and the architecture of dread". *Geoforum.* 127 (2021): 401–11.

Howard, James, director. "Episode 5". *Amazing Interiors.* 2018.

Johnson, G. Allen. "Behind the scenes of 'Host', a British horror film shot on Zoom". *Datebook.* sfchronicle.com, July 29, 2020.

Masco, Joseph. "Life Underground: Building the Bunker Society". *Anthropology Now.* 1, no. 2 (2009): 13–29.

Nemiroff, Perri. "Host Director Rob Savage Explains His Terrifying Lockdown Horror Movie: The Witching Hour," *Collider Ladies Night,* YouTube, August 14, 2020.

O'Connell, Mark. *Notes from an Apocalypse: A Personal Journey to the End of the World and Back.* Doubleday, 2020.

Osnos, Evan. "Doomsday Prep for the Super-Rich". *The New Yorker,* 26 January, 2017.

Pascuzzi, Francesco, and Sandra Waters. *The Spaces and Places of Horror.* Vernon Press, 2020.

Reuters. "U.S. 'prepper' Culture Diversifies amid Fear of Disaster and Political Unrest". NBCNews.com, 11 March, 2024.

Rymer, Russ. *Genie: A Scientific Tragedy.* Harper Perennial, 1994.

My House

McAndrew, Francis T. "The Psychology, Geography, and Architecture of Horror: How Places Creep Us Out". *Evolutionary Studies in Imaginative Culture.* 4, no. 2 (2020): 47–61.

Notes

American Houses

1. Berlant, Lauren Gail. *Cruel Optimism*. Durham, NC: Duke University Press, 2012.
2. Clark, Clifford Edward. *The American Home*.
3. Churchwell, Sarah. *Behold, America*.
4. Schudson, Michael. *American Dreams*.
5. Després, Carole. *The Meaning of Home*.
6. Dezember, Ryan. *Underwater: How Our American Dream of Homeownership Became a Nightmare*.
7. Després, Carole. "The Meaning of Home".
8. Sixsmith, Judith. "The Meaning of Home".
9. Zillow Selling. "A Haunted House? Here's What You Need to Know". zillow.com, Oct 29, 2019
10. Stambovsky v. Ackley, 169 A.D.2d 254, 572 N.Y.S.2d 672 (N.Y. App. Div. 1991)
11. Pliny, the Younger. *Letters of Pliny the Younger*.
12. Dezember, *Ryan. Underwater: How Our American Dream of Homeownership Became a Nightmare*.
13. Bachelard (xxxvii).
14. Crowely, Kieran. "Amityville' Killer Slays New Theory". *New York Post*, July 10, 2002.
15. Smith, Jennifer. "Ex-resident of house debunks much of Amityville 'horror'". *The Seattle Times*, May 8, 2005.
16. "Amityville Horror: Horror or Hoax?" abcnews.go.com, October 31, 2002.

Brutal Houses

1. The fictional Hjalmar Poelzig was modeled after the real avant-garde architect and theater set designer Hans Poelzig.
2. Heathcote, Edwin. "The architecture of horror shifts from gothic to Modernist". FT.com.
3. Sippell, Margeaux. "'I Am the Night' Team on Filming in the John Sowden House". Variety.com, January 25, 2019.
4. *Fort Wayne Sentinel*. February 26, 1912, Fort Wayne, Indiana.
5. Hawthorne, Chris. "That Far Corner: Frank Lloyd Wright in Los Angeles".
6. Hodel, Steve. *Black Dahlia Avenger: A Genius for Murder.*
7. Ibid.
8. *Fort Wayne Sentinel*, Fort Wayne, Indiana, 26 February, 1912
9. Ian Flemming hated Erno Goldfinger's brutalist buildings so much he named his most famous Bond villain after him.
10. Cilento, Karen. "Frank Lloyd Wright's Textile Houses".
11. Trufelman, Avery. "Hard to Love a Brute".
12. Ballard, J.G. *High-Rise.*
13. Easton, Kenneth. "Views on Le Corbusier's Unite d'Habitation." *Architectural Review*. 8 May, 1951.
14. Winston, Anne. "High Rise is 'not a criticism of post-war architecture'". *Dezeen.com*, 25 March 2016.
15. Ballard, J.G. *High-Rise.*
16. Miller, Joan. Pruitt-Igoe. *Survival in a Concrete Ghetto.*
17. Comerio, Mary C. "Pruitt Igoe and Other Stories".
18. Miller, Joan. *Pruitt-Igoe: Survival in a Concrete Ghetto.*
19. Cinema Tyler, *The Real Futuristic Art and Locations Kubrick Found for A Clockwork Orange.*

20. Hazzard, Jago. *Thamesmead: A Town for the Twenty-First Century*.
21. Hanson, Kitty. "Welfare Island: Stepchild with Sordid Past". *Daily News*, October 23, 1967.
22. Burgee, John & Johnson, Philip. *The Island Nobody Knows*.
23. Rus, Mayer. "Step Inside Kim Kardashian West and Kanye West's Boundary-Defying Home". *Architecturaldigest.com*, 3 February, 2020.
24. Yang, Maya. "Kanye West wanted to transform Malibu home into 'bomb shelter'". Theguardian.com, 13 September, 2023.
25. Hatherley, Owen. *Militant Modernism*.

Witch Houses

1. Grossman, Pam. *Waking the Witch: Reflections on Women, Magic, and Power*.
2. Chollet, Mona. *In Defense of Witches: the Legacy of the Witch Hunts and Why Women Are Still on Trial*.
3. Denny, Frances. *Major Arcana: Witches in America*.
4. Natali, Vincenzo. *The Architecture of Fear*, Miskatonic Institute of Horror Studies, online lecture, April 23, 2024.
5. McDonagh, Maitland. *Broken Mirrors/Broken Minds: The Dark Dreams of Dario Argento*.
6. They each have a Spice Girl–like nickname for their defining attribute: Gorgeous (Kimiko Ikegami), Fantasy (Kumiko Oba), Prof (Ai Matsubara), Sweet (Masayo Miyako), Mac (Mieko Sato), Kung Fu (Miki Jinbo), and Melody (Eriko Tanaka).
7. Perkins, Oz. "The Beautifully Grim Fairy Tale: Production Designer Jeremy Reed on *Gretel and Hansel*".
8. Comaroff, Joshua, and Ong Ker-Shin. *Horror in Architecture*.

9. With good reason. The real Los Altos Apartments, used as the exterior, housed a who's who of Hollywood royalty. Built in 1925, the mission style building was home to Clara Bow, Bette Davis, Mae West, Douglas Fairbanks, Ava Gardner, Judy Garland, and even William Randolph Hearst and Marion Davies had a two-floor suite.
10. Mendelsohn, Hadley. "How This Oceanfront Oasis Became the Most Infamous Mansion in the Hamptons".
11. Maysles, Albert, and David Maysles. directors, *Grey Gardens*, Portrait Films, 1975.
12. Ibid.
13. Sheehy, Gail. "The Secrets of Grey Gardens". *New York Magazine*, 10 January, 1972.
14. Herring, Scott. *The Hoarders: Material Deviance in Modern American Culture.*
15. Mendelsohn, Hadley. "How a Famous Author Revived a Ruined Mansion Using Vintage Design Magazines". HouseBeautiful.com, 31 August, 2022.
16. Chollet, Mona. *In Defense of Witches: The Legacy of the Witch Hunts and Why Women Are Still on Trial.*

Mad Houses

1. *Kaczynski's cabin ends long journey*, CNN, December 4, 1997.
2. Worthington, Leah. *The Man Who Shot the Unabomber Cabin.*
3. Franklin, Ruth, *Shirley Jackson: A Rather Haunted Life.*
4. Burns, Sarah. *Better for Haunts: Victorian Houses and the Modern Imagination.*
5. French, Christine Madrid. *The Architecture of Suspense: The Built World in the Films of Alfred Hitchcock.*
6. Parker, Cornelia. Transitional Object (Psychobarn).

7. Jonusas, Susan. *Hell's Half-Acre: The Untold Story of the Benders, a Serial Killer Family on the American Frontier.*
8. Comaroff, Joshua, and Ong Ker-Shing. *Horror of Architecture.*
9. Ibid.
10. *Life*, December 2, 1957.
11. Schechter, Harold. *Deviant.*
12. Ibid.
13. Ibid.
14. Ignoffo, Mary Jo. *Captive of the Labyrinth.*
15. *Winchester Mystery House as a Labyrinth*, Santa Clara University Digital Exhibits.
16. *Oakland Tribune* (Oakland, California). October 29, 1922, Sun.
17. Ignoffo, Mary Jo. *Captive of the Labyrinth: Sarah L. Winchester, Heiress to the Rifle Fortune.*

Little Houses

1. *Fangoria* magazine's 2023 Chainsaw Awards includes the category "Best Amityville," honoring the best of the years new batch of "Amityville" movies. Nominees included: *Amityville Christmas Vacation, Amityville in Space, Amityville Karen, Amityville Scarecrow II*, and *Amityville Uprising.*
2. Ramalho, Joana Rita. *Creepy Dolls: From Precious Playthings to Harbingers of Death*, Miskatonic Institute of Horror Studies, online lecture, October 21, 2021.
3. Garfield, Simon. *In Miniature.*
4. An image that contains a smaller version of itself, suggesting an infinitely recurred sequence of images each smaller than the other..

5. Lagacé, Rose. "Production Designer John Paino Gives Us an Insightful New Look at Sharp Objects". *Art Departmental*, 17 April, 2020.

6. Ibid.

7. Botz, Corinne May. *The Nutshell Studies of Unexplained Death.*

8. Ibid.

9. Ibid.

10. Weisstuch, Liza. "Jobless, Divorced, on Probation; a Pandemic Hobby Turned His Life Around". NYtimes.com, September 8, 2023.

Forever Houses

1. "Chilling Cold War Moments". *LA Times,* October 30, 2006

2. Hewitt, Chris, "Down in the Bunker". *Empire Magazine*, August 2016

3. Terravivos.com.

4. Garrett, Bradley. "Doomsday preppers and the architecture of dread".

5. Howard, James, director. *Amazing Interiors*, ep. 5, Netflix, 2018.

6. O'Connell, Mark. *Notes from an Apocalypse: A Personal Journey to the End of the World and Back.*

7. Fisher, Mark. "Dogtooth: The Family Syndrome". *Film Quarterly*. 64, No. 4 (Summer 2011) 22–7.

8. Rymer, Russ. *Genie: A Scientific Tragedy.*

9. Johnson, G. Allen. "Behind the scenes of 'Host', a British horror film shot on Zoom". *Datebook*, sfchronicle.com, July 29, 2020.

10. Nemiroff, Perri. "Host Director Rob Savage Explains His Terrifying Lockdown Horror Movie: The Witching Hour". *Collider Ladies Night*, YouTube, August 14, 2020.

DARKLY

BLACK HISTORY AND

AMERICA'S GOTHIC SOUL

by Leila Taylor

Haunted houses, bitter revenants and muffled heartbeats under floorboards — the American gothic is a macabre tale based on a true story.

Part memoir and part cultural critique, *Darkly* reveals the heart of America's darkness in the specters left from chattel slavery and the persistence of white supremacy. Locating the gothic in technologies of terror, the insurgency of melancholy, and the guilty conscience of a country that got away with murder, *Darkly* shows how this trauma has been metabolized into art, music, film, and literature.

America's story is founded in horror, with a culture shaped from the Black experience, proving that you can't get more goth than Black.

Order online from <u>RepeaterBooks.com</u>

HAUNTED STATES

AN AMERICAN GOTHIC GUIDEBOOK

by Miranda Corcoran

Haunted States is a unique guidebook that explores the dark, often horrifying, history of the US. Based on the author's journey across the United States in summer 2022, it explores locations connected to Gothic fiction and film, tracking the relationship between the American landscapes and the various forms of fictional horror the nation has produced over the centuries.

Part cultural history and part travelogue, *Haunted States* traces how the American Gothic draws inspiration from the natural and built environments, with the astounding geographical variation of the landscape influencing the distinctive forms of horror produced across its many diverse regions. The book also investigates how the horrors of the American Gothic have their roots in the nation's dark history of colonialism, slavery, violence and oppression – past sins that continue to haunt the national consciousness to this day.

Order online from RepeaterBooks.com

CORPSES, FOOLS, & MONSTERS

THE HISTORY AND FUTURE

OF TRANSNESS IN CINEMA

by Willow Maclay and Caden Gardner

In the history of cinema, trans people are usually murdered, made into a joke, or viewed as threats to the normal order — relegated to a lost highway of corpses, fools, and monsters.

In this book, trans film critics Caden Mark Gardner and Willow Catelyn Maclay take the reader on a drive down this lost highway, exploring the way that trans people and transness have evolved on-screen. Starting from the very earliest representations of transness in silent film, through to the multiplex-conquering Matrix franchise and on to the emergence of a true trans-authored cinema, *Corpses, Fools, and Monsters* spans everything from musicals to body horror to avant garde experimental film to tell the story of the trans film image.

THE REPEATER BOOK OF THE OCCULT

TALES FROM THE DARKSIDE

by Euguene Thacker and Tariq Goddard

Edited by novelist and Repeater publisher Tariq Goddard and "horror philosopher" Eugene Thacker, *The Repeater Book of the Occult* is a new anthology of horror stories that explores the ever-shifting boundaries between the natural and supernatural, between the real and the unreal. As the editors note, "In the grey zone between what appears and what is, lies horror. But horror writing is also a certain disposition, a way of thinking based on a suspicion regarding the world as it is given to us, and a doubt regarding the accepted ways of explaining that world to us – and for us."

The Repeater Book of the Occult includes introductions by Repeater authors such as Leila Taylor, Carl Neville, Rhian E Jones, and Elvia Wilk, and features horror classics by Algernon Blackwood, Charlotte Perkins Gilman, and Edgar Allan Poe, as well as forgotten gems by authors such as W.W. Jacobs, Mark Twain, and Sheridan Le Fanu.

Order online from RepeaterBooks.com

REPEATER BOOKS

is dedicated to the creation of a new reality. The landscape of twenty-first-century arts and letters is faded and inert, riven by fashionable cynicism, egotistical self-reference and a nostalgia for the recent past. Repeater intends to add its voice to those movements that wish to enter history and assert control over its currents, gathering together scattered and isolated voices with those who have already called for an escape from Capitalist Realism. Our desire is to publish in every sphere and genre, combining vigorous dissent and a pragmatic willingness to succeed where messianic abstraction and quiescent co-option have stalled: abstention is not an option: we are alive and we don't agree.